MALABOCH

MALABOCH

OR

NOTES FROM MY DIARY ON

THE BOER CAMPAIGN OF 1894

AGAINST THE CHIEF MALABOCH

OF BLAAUWBERG, DISTRICT ZOUTPANSBERG,
SOUTH AFRICAN REPUBLIC

TO WHICH IS APPENDED

A SYNOPSIS OF

THE JOHANNESBURG CRISIS OF 1896

BY

THE REV. COLIN RAE

LATE CHAPLAIN TO THE MALABOCH FORCES.

WITH ILLUSTRATIONS

LONDON
SAMPSON LOW, MARSTON AND COMPANY
LIMITED
St. Dunstan's House, Fetter Lane, Fleet Street, E.C.

SOUTH AFRICA
J. C. JUTA & CO.
CAPE TOWN, PORT ELIZABETH, JOHANNESBURG,
STELLENBOSCH

1898

TO

THE OFFICERS, NON-COMMISSIONED OFFICERS,
AND TROOPERS

OF

THE PRETORIA CONTINGENT

AS A TRIBUTE OF CORDIAL FRIENDSHIP;
AND IN ADMIRATION OF THEIR CONDUCT
IN THE CAMP AND THE FIELD
DURING THE EXPEDITION AGAINST MALABOCH,
THE FOLLOWING NARRATIVE

is affectionately inscribed

BY

THE AUTHOR.

PREFACE.

In presenting the following account to the indulgence of the public, I am keeping a promise made to my comrades in the Malaboch compaign, who were kind enough to think that a published diary of events would be of interest, not only to those who were engaged in the expedition, but to a larger number who watched the proceedings of each day with anxiety, and who are deeply interested in South African affairs generally.

The circumstances under which I accompanied the forces as chaplain require some explanation.

The Bishop's choice lay between the Rev. J. W. Llewelyn (then in Maraisburg) and myself.

The Rev. Canon Fisher, D.D., had also volunteered his services, but there were obstacles in the way which prevented his going.

Being on the spot, and holding but a temporary appointment in Pretoria, the choice fell upon me. His Lordship had removed me from Fordsburg (in deference to my wishes) only a few days before the declaration of war.

The success of my ministry amongst the troops (for which I have been, and shall always be humbly grateful) was chiefly due to the faithful prayers of friends and well-wishers.

The sudden death of poor Tobias affected me in more ways than one.

He was special correspondent for the *Volkstem*, Pretoria, and when writing his despatches used multigraph copying-books. He invariably read these despatches to me before sending them away, and promised, on our return to Pretoria, to present me with a complete English translation; but his untimely death prevented this arrangement. Depending on these notes, I did not take such minute particulars as I should otherwise have done, and I am indebted to the *Press* for some details of engagements and incidents recorded herein which the doctor had better opportunity of obtaining than I had. I have to thank Mr. Mauritz Preller for supplying me with the copies of the *Press*.

With regard to Mr. Anthony Vlotman's verbatim narrative, entitled "The Real Cause of the War," I am at variance with him upon one point. Mr. Vlotman prefaces his statement by saying that Malaboch had never paid taxes since 1881. This, however, is open to question, as I have received information to the contrary from other, not less reliable, sources. Yet, be this as it may, the policy of the Government in subduing these petty chiefs is for the future good of the country, and the general advancement of the native races.

As long as the power vested in the Government is used in bringing out the Kafirs from their strongholds of laziness to work for the advancement of *all classes* of industry in the State, so long will it have the countenance of enlightened men.

It has been stated, in connection with the Johannesburg crisis, that the leaders of the Reform party were playing with fire, and knew not the possible consequences of their acts; but it is fair to add that they knew the possible consequences of their acts with regard to commerce, as the following list will prove; a relief fund having been opened and liberally subscribed to, with the view of compensating those poorer inhabitants of Johannesburg who might be injuriously affected in their commercial or other position in life by the movement:—

	£
The Consolidated Goldfields . . .	15,000
S. Neumann & Co.	10,000
H. Eckstein & Co.	10,000
George Farrar	10,000
Barnato Bros.	10,000
Lionel Phillips	5,000
Abe Bailey	5,000
Lace & Thompson	5,000
H. B. Marshall	2,000
Lingham Timber Syndicate (Limited) .	1,000
W. D. Davis	1,000
Fehr & Dubois	1,000
Making a total of . .	75,000

In conclusion, I must acknowledge my deep sense of gratitude to friends who have helped in making this work *un fait accompli*. To Mrs. C. Bancroft, Miss Edythe E. Townsend, and Mr. Fred Neel, for rendering valuable artistic aid. Messrs. W. K. Packman, A. C. Alder, and C. F. Alston, for assisting in the wearisome task of transcription, I tender my sincere thanks. Particularly am I indebted to Mr. R. H. Willson, who wrote the whole of 'Malaboch' in its rough stage, from my dictation, in his residence, "the house in Pilgrim's Creek," and to Mr. Dan Matthews, for his indefatigable labours in assisting in the revision.

Those who have compiled a similar work will understand the real value of such help.

Situated, as I am, in the midst of a mining camp, where the population is scattered over an area of many miles, the calls made upon my time are varied and frequent; consequently, I have not been able to devote that care I could have desired to the literary portion of the work.

I, therefore, submit this volume to the lenient criticism of the reader.

THE AUTHOR. [*To face page* xi.

CONTENTS.

CHAPTER I.
OFF TO THE WAR	PAGE 1

CHAPTER II.
A DILEMMA	10

CHAPTER III.
A DISORDERLY CAMP	17

CHAPTER IV.
A DAY'S HUNTING	20

CHAPTER V.
THE WARM BATHS	24

CHAPTER VI.
A DESERTER	28

CHAPTER VII.
A NOCTURNAL FLITTING—THE MALABOCH WAR SONG	33

CHAPTER VIII.
THE REVEREND MR. PARISIUS	44

CONTENTS

CHAPTER IX.
AN INTERESTING DAY 49

CHAPTER X.
THE FIRST SKIRMISH 55

CHAPTER XI.
I SPEND A NIGHT ON FORT HOLZER KOPJE . . . 63

CHAPTER XII.
THE COMMISSARIAT 69

CHAPTER XIII.
MY FIRST EXPERIENCE UNDER FIRE 73

CHAPTER XIV.
FIRST CASUALTIES 79

CHAPTER XV.
THE FIRST FUNERAL 85

CHAPTER XVI.
THE COLONEL'S DREAM 95

CHAPTER XVII.
THE CAPTURE OF CATTLE 98

CHAPTER XVIII.
THE REVEREND C. SONNTAG 104

CHAPTER XIX.
I VISIT THE PRETORIA FORT 113

CHAPTER XX.

MORE CASUALTIES—DEATH OF SCHMIDT 124

CHAPTER XXI.

THE HOSPITAL 133

CHAPTER XXII.

HONOUR TO WHOM HONOUR IS DUE 138

CHAPTER XXIII.

THE CHIEF MEDICAL OFFICER 145

CHAPTER XXIV.

THE TERRIBLE DEATH OF GROENEWALD—MR. FRED NEEL MEETS WITH AN ACCIDENT 156

CHAPTER XXV.

A COURT-MARTIAL 160

CHAPTER XXVI.

ACCIDENT TO CAPTAIN STENT—THE COMMISSARY-GENERAL . 164

CHAPTER XXVII.

NEARING THE END—SURRENDER OF WOMEN AND CHILDREN —MALABOCH SPEAKS 168

CHAPTER XXVIII.

A NIGHT ON THE MOUNTAIN IN THE MOONLIGHT—MR. JENKINS' PICNIC PARTY 173

CHAPTER XXIX.

THE SURRENDER OF MALABOCH 177

CHAPTER XXX.

THE HOSPITAL STAFF—A COUNCIL OF WAR . . . 184

CHAPTER XXXI.

HOMEWARD BOUND 189

CHAPTER XXXII.

TRIUMPHAL ENTRY INTO PRETORIA—THE RECEPTION COMMITTEE—THE PRESIDENT'S SPEECH 199

CHAPTER XXXIII.

THE ARRIVAL OF MALABOCH IN PRETORIA — DEATH OF DR. TOBIAS—ST. AUGUSTINE'S BROTHERHOOD—I GO TO ROODEPOORT, AND FROM THENCE TO PILGRIM'S REST . 205

GLOSSARY 215

APPENDIX.

THE JOHANNESBURG CRISIS 219

LIST OF ILLUSTRATIONS.

THE AUTHOR	To face p.	xi
THE CHIEF, MALABOCH	,,	xvii
THE RIGHT REV. HENRY BROUGHAM BOUSFIELD, D.D., FIRST BISHOP OF PRETORIA	,,	2
THE HOUSE IN PILGRIM'S CREEK, PILGRIMS' REST, WHERE "MALABOCH" WAS WRITTEN	,,	5
THE DEPARTURE OF THE PRETORIA COMMANDO	,,	6
COMMANDANT HIS HONOUR GENERAL P. J. JOUBERT	,,	8
COLONEL FERREIRA, C.M.G.	,,	11
VELD-CORNET PIET KRUGER	,,	11
COMMANDANT MALAN	,,	11
ADJUTANT S. J. ELOFF AND SERGEANT-MAJOR J. MALAN	,,	12
MESS NO. 2	,,	14
MESS NO. 3	,,	17
LIEUTENANT J. SCHROEDER	,,	20
THE PRETORIA HORSE IN FRONT OF BLAAUWBERG	,,	22
OFFICERS AND NON-COMMISSIONED OFFICERS OF THE PRETORIA TOWN CONTINGENT	,,	29
MAMATOLLA	,,	51
PRETORIA TOWN PATROLS	,,	51
TROOPER T. H. MCARTHUR	,,	58
LIEUTENANT HOLZER	,,	65
STAATS ARTILLERY: SHOWING THE MAXIMS	,,	66
GENERAL VIEW OF BLAAUWBERG FROM THE PIETERSBURG LAAGER	,,	88
BURIAL OF BURGHER NEL—THE FIRST FUNERAL	,,	90
REV. C. SONNTAG'S RESIDENCE	,,	90
THE COMMANDEERED PRISONERS AND THEIR GUARDS	,,	113
STAATS ARTILLERY CAMP: BLAAUWBERG IN BACKGROUND	,,	114

LIST OF ILLUSTRATIONS

Plan of proposed Blowing-up of Maláboch's Caves	*To face p.*	117
Acting Veld-Cornet Charles Rice	,,	145
Dr. Jameson	,,	145
Maláboch at Bay	,,	169
Mementos found in Hoofdstad	,,	182
The late Commandant Henning Pretorius	,,	186
Address of Welcome	,,	202
His Honour S. J. P. Kruger State President Z.A.R.	,,	204
Mr. Ewald Esselen (late State Attorney)	,,	206
Dr. W. J. Leyds (late State Secretary)	,,	208
The State Prisoner, Maláboch, in the Pretoria Gaol	,,	210
Metamorphosed Warriors	,,	212
Comrades of the late Dr. Tobias (just before the Funeral)	,,	214
The late Reverend Father Douglas, S.S.J.	,,	216
St. Augustine's Brotherhood, Modderpoort, Ladybrand, O.F.S.	,,	218
Letter from Mr. Ewald Esselen	,,	220
St. Mary's Church, Pilgrim's Rest	,,	222
Pilgrim's Rest Mining Camp (from the West) District Lydenburg	,,	224
Church of St. John the Evangelist, Lydenburg	,,	228
Excitement in Johannesburg, outside the Goldfields Buildings	,,	230
The Offices of the Reform Committee	,,	232
The late Lord Rosmead (Sir Hercules Robinson)	,,	234
Residence of Mr. H. Hellman, Mariasburg	,,	236
Troopers' Grave at Doornkop	,,	238
Refugees fleeing from Johannesburg	,,	240
The Great Reform Trial at Pretoria	,,	242
The late Mr. B. I. Barnato	,,	244
Cartridges, Vultures' Feathers, Spent Bullet, Ramrod, and Necktie from Doornkop	,,	246
Map of the Scene of War	*At end.*	

THE CHIEF, MALABOCH.
(*After a photograph taken in Pretoria Gaol by Leo. Weinthal.*)

[*To face page* **xvii**.

INTRODUCTION.

THE REAL CAUSE OF THE WAR.

Mr. Anthony Vlotman's verbatim Narrative.

AFTER the Transvaal was given back to the Boers by the British in 1881, Malaboch refused to pay taxes to the new Government, and since then has never paid.

In December, 1891, Mr. Barend Vorster, Native Commissioner of Malitse's Land, with twenty-one men, including myself, proceeded to Blaauwberg, the stronghold of the recalcitrant Chief, for the purpose of collecting taxes, and encamped at the foot of the mountain, close to the Rev. C. Sonntag's mission station. The Commissioner sent some of the missionary Kafirs up to the Hoofdstad with a request for Malaboch to come down, as he wanted to take the census of the tribe. The Commissioner, with four or five men, then went a little way up the mountain, when a shot was fired at them from above. The party, without returning the fire, at once came down again to the encampment. The mission Kafirs returned the same day, with an impudent message from the Chief in these exact words: "I am baas upon this mountain, and shall not allow the census to be taken." The next morning we saw Kafirs coming down the mountain in all directions. They seized my horse and that of another of our men, which were grazing in the bush. They took them up the mountain, tying them to a tree just under the highest peak. We should not have known where the horses were had we not seen them being led away by the Kafirs. They were eventually recovered. Ten of Malaboch's head Indunas then came down and interviewed the Commissioner, and about mid-day we were completely surrounded by considerably over two thousand Kafirs variously armed with guns and assegais, though chiefly guns. I ought to mention that at that time the Chiefs Mapen and Kiviet were with Malaboch and were hostile to the Government, but they have since, as you know, become loyal supporters of the Transvaal Government, and rendered us valuable assistance during the late campaign.

Before the interview the Commissioner requested the Indunas to leave their guns on the other side of the hedge, which they did. Some Kafirs, however, were stopped when nearing the spot chosen for the interview, and told to retire to a distance with their arms, and only to approach the Commissioner unarmed. But one Kafir came within the prescribed limits with his gun, and, on the Commissioner personally telling him to go away, he refused.

The Indunas were most insolent during the whole proceedings, and all our men stood to their guns, as we quite expected to be massacred. The armed

Kafirs were only about thirty yards away, scattered in the dense bush. The interview ended about an hour before sunset, and then they brought nine of the most wretchedly miserable bullocks they could procure, and on presenting them to the Commissioner, the head Induna said: "These nine bullocks represent a pinch of snuff from Malaboch to the Transvaal Government." The same Induna then repeated Malaboch's words, that they did not intend paying any taxes, as they were the rightful owners of the mountain, and not the Boers. The Commissioner told the Indunas to tell Malaboch that that was the last appeal the Government intended to make for taxes. The Kafirs then retired, and in doing so made a big demonstration by blowing their "walt hoorns" (war horns), and firing their guns in the air at intervals.

I know the Zoutpansberg district well, having lived there on and off since the 4th February, 1888. I am well acquainted with the ways of the Kafirs, and their roguish and thieving propensities in dealing with the cattle of the Boers.

Much has been said with regard to the justice or otherwise of the Malaboch War, but I think the foregoing narrative of facts points to a sufficient *casus belli*.

MALABOCH

CHAPTER I.

OFF TO THE WAR.

The talk of Pretoria for more than a week had been the question of commandeering men for action against the rebel Chief Malaboch of Blaauwberg fame. Whenever two friends met in the street, the first greeting invariably was—" Have you been commandeered ? "

All classes were absorbed in the burning question of the hour. Indeed, it would have been utterly impossible for anyone to have overlooked it, as the appointed officers had been and were still busily pursuing their thankless task. This gave rise to much ill-feeling and dissatisfaction, and many vowed vengeance on the Government, using threats which they never intended carrying out. This feeling, however, was not shared by the whole of the community, for many of the youthful members were most eager to be numbered amongst those fortunate and lucky individuals (such they considered them) whose names had already been enrolled on the list. They even asked the Veld-Cornet to have their names added, and so sure were they of being accepted, that they had actually selected their outfit. Would the ubiquitous and indefatigable "Melt" (Veld-Cornet) pass them over? This was their only anxiety.

Not only were men commandeered, but money, provisions, and clothing were also largely requisitioned from the proprietors of all the business houses, who, to their credit, be it said, showed their loyalty to the State by giving most cheerfully the goods demanded, and, in most cases, promising to reinstate their employés should they have the good fortune to return in safety. Some of those commandeered found substitutes, to whom they paid from £30 to £60, besides providing horses, saddles, and bridles, and glad enough they were to get out of it at that price.

In the midst of all this excitement and confusion, the Bishop of Pretoria (Dr. Bousfield) was calmly considering how he could provide for the spiritual wants of the men, and on my return to luncheon a brief note from his lordship awaited me. It ran as follows :—

Saturday, May 19, 1894.

DEAR MR. RAE,—Come and see me as soon as possible.

H. B. PRETOR.

I lost no time in acceding to this request, having but little doubt as to its purport. It was, as I conjectured, to consult me as to my willingness to accompany the troops, and act as Chaplain if so required. He warned me of all dangers likely to be incurred, as well as the hardships likely to be endured. I immediately consented, as these did not deter me, promising to be ready to start at half a day's notice.

[*To face page* 2.

THE RIGHT REV. HENRY BROUGHAM BOUSFIELD, D.D.,
FIRST BISHOP OF PRETORIA.

On the following Monday the Veld-Cornet's office presented a scene of wild excitement. Hundreds of men were waiting to interview the sturdy official, Mr. Melt Marais. To many this would have proved somewhat distracting, but he stood his ground and would accept of no excuses. He was determined to do his duty, and right well he did it too. He was not a little surprised to find so many of his fellow-townsmen suffering from all kinds of chronic disorders, numerous medical certificates being produced to such effect. Sons, who were the sole support of their widowed mothers, were there in large numbers. Even Burghers of the State were present making excuses in order to be exempted from active service. But the hard-hearted "Melt" was not to be cajoled. The law had to be enforced, and go they must. Some of the more sensible had grasped the situation, and were, in the absence of all order or system, hauling over the rifles and selecting their choice. It was a strange scene, and, to some extent, amusing.

After making many calls at the office, which took up the greater part of the day, I at last succeeded in catching the eye of Mr. Marais, and, beckoning him, begged a few moments of his valuable time. Without prefacing my remarks, I went to the subject at issue at once, and asked for a horse, saddle, bridle, revolver, rifle, and ammunition, all of which I considered absolutely necessary for my equipment. But my modest requests were just as promptly though politely declined; being informed at the same time that the Government only saw its way to supply me with rations. The matter thus being settled, I next turned my thoughts towards my outfit, and wended my way down Church Street. Being in a dilemma as to what would be required, I consulted Canon Fisher, an old campaigner through the Bechuanaland war, who kindly supplied me with a list and presented me with several useful articles which he had himself used. Armed with this list, I was proceeding to make my own purchases when, luckily, I encountered Mr. Mogg, a well-known and highly respected gentleman in Pretoria. With such a pioneer my troubles were much lessened, for taking me to the "Ready Money" Outfitting Establishment, he purchased some of the goods, for which he generously refused to accept payment. This was not by any means my only experience of the generosity of the residents in Pretoria—Mr. Thomas B. Burnham, the senior warden of the cathedral, and the members of his house were most kind; Mr. Burnham not only gave me good advice with regard to camp life, but showed his kindness in a more practical manner, by providing me with warm clothing and a camp-chair, while Mrs. Burnham and family sent a large box of dainties weighing about sixty pounds. From Mr. and Mrs. Henshall I received a box of similar weight, containing groceries, fresh and preserved vegetables, and medicines. A lady, whose name I have unfortunately forgotten, sent a sum of money through Mr. Burnham. Mrs. Fisher and the late Mrs. Mogg were most energetic in gathering subscriptions, with the result

THE HOUSE IN PILGRIM'S CREEK, PILGRIM'S REST, Z.A.R., WHERE "MALABOCH" WAS WRITTEN.
(Photographed by George Damant, from a sketch by Edythe E. Townsend.)

[To face page 5.

that a cheque for eleven pounds was posted on to me after my arrival at Blaauwberg. The Bishop, too, assisted me, so that I was put to very little expense myself.

To all who so generously rendered assistance I tender my deepest gratitude.

The day before starting, the Uitlander's Association held a public meeting in the Caledonian Hall, which was packed to overflowing long before the appointed hour; the chief object being to enlist the sympathy of the public on behalf of the five political prisoners, Messrs. Reno, Maynard, Clarke, Steer, and Ingle, and to collect subscriptions for their defence against the State prosecution, they having refused point blank to comply with the demands of the law in the matter of being commandeered for service.

Indignation meetings had also been held on Church Square during the day, where much was said though little was done. On my way to Bishop's Cote in the evening, I noticed that the streets were quite deserted—only at the Caledonian Hall was there any excitement. The Bishop had arranged for a special service in his unique and pretty little private chapel, situated in the episcopal grounds, which, by the way, is built of Willesden paper, and had already stood the test of several wet seasons, and was but little the worse for wear. I found the Bishop in his study, and soon after my arrival an adjournment was made to the chapel, where we were joined by the late Rev. R. J. P. Dunbar of the cathedral, Mrs. Bousfield, and the Misses Bousfield. On my return home, late as it was, I found Mrs. Sinclair, my worthy hostess, busily engaged in packing my trunk; the kindness of this lady and her family to me will be long remembered. Early next morning a special service for churchmen commandeered was held in the cathedral, and the Holy Communion celebrated by the Bishop. Special prayers compiled by his lordship were said, in which the Rulers of the State, the commandeered, and myself were remembered. During the morning Mr. E. F. Simpsom called on behalf of the Hospital Comforts Committee, and invited me to the Union Club, where a meeting was being held. There I was introduced to Messrs. C. Ueckerman, S. Jones, W. C. Schappert, Dr. Engelenberg, Colonel Ferreira, and other gentlemen who had spared no pains or trouble in providing a supply of stores for the hospital department. Through their exertions a wagon load of real comforts was procured, and I was asked to act as a member of the committee. I can assure these gentlemen that the stores were faithfully distributed without stint or favour to any who really needed such. Many a poor fellow who partook of them during the campaign had need to be deeply grateful, and I am only expressing the wishes of all my comrades (especially the sick and wounded) when I say we thank you heartily, kind friends.

The time was now drawing near for a start to be made, and the men began to muster on Church Square, each man, equipped with a Martini-Henri rifle, a bandolier well filled with ammunition, a belt and canteen, presented a most warlike ap-

THE DEPARTURE OF THE PRETORIA COMMANDO.
General Joubert addressing the Troops.

pearance. The Veld-Cornet's office was still besieged by youths who were anxious to go as substitutes. The crowd which had assembled was the largest, it was said, ever seen in Pretoria. The platform over the porch of the Government buildings was occupied by the Members of the Volksraad and their friends, whilst every available balcony was filled with eager onlookers, of whom the fair sex formed a goodly proportion. Cabs were dashing about in all directions, and the wagons of war were in readiness. Some of the men had little idea of what was required, as evidenced by their general get up, a loud check suit, straw hat, and tennis shoes, with cartridge belt put on upside down, scarcely betokened a knowledge of what should constitute a smart military appearance. One fellow had his gun-strap so mixed up with that of his canteen that it would have taken him some time to "present arms." Others took no rations with them whatever, but laughingly remarked that they did not intend to starve nevertheless. The Boers were all mounted; many of the Pretoria town contingent, however (mostly Englishmen), had no horses, and preferred keeping to the wagons rather than do stable duty.

As the clock struck four the roll was called by Lieutenant J. Schroeder, and when all had answered to their names the order was given to "quick march." Headed by the band and a detachment of the volunteers, the commando marched to the front of the Raadzaal, when the Commandant-General from the balcony addressed the men; having announced that they were to encamp at Wonderboom Poort for two days, he spoke in complimentary terms of the inhabitants of Pretoria for so nobly responding to the call of duty, and he was glad to state that almost every man who had been commandeered had resolved to take up arms to defend the land he lived in. He wished them God-speed on their perilous mission, and trusted they would all return safe and sound, and in as good health and spirits as they appeared to be on the eve of their departure, and after quoting Lord Nelson's well-known words, "The State expects that every man will do his duty," he withdrew. Great cheering followed the conclusion of the speech, and the horsemen and wagons then proceeded down Church Street bound for Wonderboom Poort. Both sides of the thoroughfare were closely packed with spectators, and almost every member of the fair sex resident was present to bid farewell to the departing warriors. Deafening cheers were raised and hats and handkerchiefs waved aloft with frantic vigour. One young fellow caused great amusement by his general bearing; he was regardlessly got up *à la militaire* in a tight-fitting kharki suit and marched along beside wagon number ——: he was evidently aware of his smart appearance and consequently carried his head erect; but, alas! he met with a dire catastrophe. Just at one of the most prominent corners, as he was attempting to get into the wagon, a side seam of his trousers burst open from top to bottom, exposing his manly leg to view; he lost no time in losing himself to sight in the interior of the wagon,

COMMANDANT, HIS HONOUR GENERAL P. J. JOUBERT.

and although it was a best on record, he was not sufficiently quick to prevent an uproarious laugh from the crowd.

Numbers of horsemen and vehicles swelled the procession until Aapies River drift was reached, when the majority of them returned together with the volunteers.

Many carriages were gathered at various points outside the town, and cheers were given by the occupants of a passing railway train.

The greatest enthusiasm prevailed, everyone being in the highest of spirits. Out of the one hundred and seventy-five men commandeered only seventeen failed to answer to their names, eight of whom turned up later on, while the others were in the wagons asleep.

Darkness had set in when we reached our rendezvous, and for some hours all was activity and disorder. There were some final and pathetic leave-takings at this spot, and after something like quiet and order were obtained, Lieutenant Charles Rice was appointed Commandant for the night. Furnishing myself with a rug and waterproof sheet, I retired for the night under the wagon by the side of Sergeant Lovell Taylor, and slept as soundly as I should have done in my comfortable bed in the house of Mrs. Sinclair in Proes Street.

CHAPTER II.

A DILEMMA.

I AROSE at six the next morning, and after going through my ablutions in the river close by, we received orders from headquarters to proceed to the Thorns, and reached there at nightfall. An unknown friend kindly sent me the daily papers. To-day, being the anniversary of Her Majesty Queen Victoria's birthday, we sang the National Anthem in honour of the occasion, and three loud, ringing cheers were given by Her Gracious Majesty's loyal subjects, who, although resident thousands of miles away from their native soil, were as hearty and sincere in their congratulations as any Britisher could wish to be. I may state that, during the five years I have lived in South Africa, I have invariably noticed how thoroughly devoted and attached the British subjects are to their Sovereign.

It was raining hard when the acting Veld-Cornet called the roll; wagons with burghers were constantly swelling our ranks. While on our way here we had to commandeer a "voorlooper," the boy who had been acting in that capacity not being in a fit state to lead the oxen. Our new voorlooper, being thus suddenly kidnapped, was apparently much frightened, and would have liked to run away, but

VELD-CORNET PIET KRUGER,
Rustenburg Contingent.

COLONEL FERREIRA, C.M.G.,
Veld-Cornet, Pretoria Contingent.

COMMANDANT MALAN,
Rustenburg Burgher Contingent.

[To face page 11.

dared not. The rains came on heavily just about this time, and we were in a most deplorable state, having neither bucksail nor tent; these had been promised, but had not yet arrived. A meeting was held in the rain, at which Colonel Ferreira was unanimously elected Acting-Commandant for the Pretoria Town Contingent, and he in turn appointed Lieutenant Sarel Eloff as second in command. We, that is to say No. 2 mess, then retired for the night inside the wagon, leaving Messrs. Malan and Conradie on guard. The discomfort to which we were put may be imagined, when I state that the accommodation thus afforded was scarcely sufficient for four, let alone twelve, for the two came off guard at midnight wet through, and we were literally packed like so many sardines. I have never before, nor since, experienced such inconvenience in my sleeping quarters. One could not stretch one's legs for fear of kicking somebody's head, and constant cries were heard, such as, "Oh, do take your feet away!" "Steady, man, that's my head!" "Hang it all, give a fellow a little more room!" "Who's that with a boot on?" It was I who had to plead guilty to the latter. Before retiring I was standing by the wagon in my top-boots in the pouring rain. I was afraid to stir, as every time I moved I gathered a fresh clod of the glutinous potclay, which stuck to me with a leechlike tenacity aggravating in the extreme. The consequence was, I had to sleep with one boot on, for do what I would I could not get it off, and the poor fellow whose head it had come in contact with was naturally highly indignant, and many were the tugs given by my enraged comrades during the course of the night to relieve me of this refractory boot, but without success, so I remained, like the old woman in the song, "with one boot off and the other boot on," and was perforce compelled to listen in silence to the smothered abjurgations of my incensed friends. Little did I think when parting with my thirty-five shillings for these "snake-bite protectors" that they would so soon be the means of bringing me into such an undignified position. We welcomed the daybreak with delight, and when revèille was sounded by Bugler Fuchs, we lost no time in emerging from our cramped and close quarters to straighten our crooked limbs, and to inhale the fresh breezes of heaven, although it was still raining hard, and the soil just as aggravatingly tenacious as ever. Before proceeding further, I will here give the names of those who formed No. 2 mess, which I had joined :—Lieutenant Sarel Eloff, Adjutant; Sergeant-Major Jonathan Malan ; Sergeants Lovell Taylor and Anthony Vlotman ; Corporal Gert Botha, in charge of the wagon ; Corporal Frans Conradie ; Troopers Austin Brook, Mauritz Preller, Durbin Brice, Charles Dargan, and Jacques du Toit; and a most amiable set of fellows they all were. They spared no pains in making me as comfortable as they possibly could, and the whole of the contingent displayed admirable good temper under most unpleasant and trying circumstances ; they realised their position, and were prepared for difficulties, therefore they

SERGEANT-MAJOR J. MALAN. ADJUTANT S. J. ELOFF.

fully understood how utterly foolish it would have been to grumble at the inevitable. The camp was situated on the bank of the Aapies River, close to the Thorns Hotel. It was unfortunate, however, that the spot chosen was not the best that might have been selected, the ground being of a spongy and turfy nature, which made it a most unsuitable place to pitch tents in wet weather.

The wagons were soon inspanned, and the horses saddled, but alas! number "two" was in a dilemma. Three of the oxen were either lost, stolen, or strayed; we had not a full span to start with (only ten), and they were very poor. We were, therefore, left with seven trek oxen, and an old black cow; the latter was given us as we were leaving Pretoria by Mr. Celliers for slaughtering. This animal was pressed into the service and inspanned; we had the greatest difficulty in moving the wagon, the wheels being embedded deep down in the yielding turf. After proceeding a few yards, the cow slipped her head from the yoke, and fled with a most remarkable speed until she was lost to sight, and we saw her no more. All the other wagons had gone on, and were now out of sight. We had to take the odd ox out, and try to get along with the remaining six; but this was utterly impossible, more especially as we were without a whip; the only thing we could do was to wait. A new idea, however, struck us: Could not we commandeer three oxen? But from whom, and where? Durbin Brice, the youngest member of our mess, armed with his rifle, left the wagon, and began to explore. He returned in a short time, driving before him three very good beasts which he had seized from a kraal close by. They were soon inspanned with the others, and having secured a whip by the same means from a passing wagon, we were able to proceed.

It was now getting late, and darkness had begun to set in. The roads were in a horrible condition, simply one mass of slush; and as our voorlooper was ignorant of the way, Mauritz Preller, after divesting himself of most of his clothing, took his place. I do not know how we should have fared had he not done so. He trudged through the slush for hours whooping and yelling, until we came to a place called the Pyramids. Here we brought our wagon to a standstill, and arranged our sleeping quarters for the night, and had supper. We were suffering from a burning thirst, but our water-barrels and canteens were all empty, with the exception of mine, which contained about half a pint of water. This had to serve for the ablutions of Mauritz, who was in a fearful state, being covered with mud from head to foot, and almost fainting from fatigue. After wrapping him up in blankets, we retired for the night. Four of our number, namely, Messrs. Eloff, Malan, Vlotman, and Conradie, had gone on with the horsemen. This gave us more room, and we were soon comfortably settled in the wagon, and slept soundly. I should here mention that, by this time, the refractory boot had at last come off, and was now hanging with its companion alongside the wagon, and, needless to say, there it remained.

L. TAYLOR. A. BROOKE. G. BOTHA. J. DUTOIT. A. VLÆTMAN. C. DARGAN.
REV. COLIN RAE. F. CONRADIE. M. PREILER.
D. BRICE. MESS No. 2.

[To face page 14.

We trekked at 7.15 next morning to Waterval, where we were joined by our four comrades who had left the advance column to find out our whereabouts. They condoled with us in our misfortunes, and we then sat down to breakfast—a meal we thoroughly enjoyed, especially the coffee, for we had not yet been able to satisfy our thirst of the previous night. Many purchases were made here, and we afterwards trekked on entering the bush-veld at 4.30 P.M., and reaching Haman's Kraal at five. Here we rested, intending to stop for the night, and I sent a telegram to the Bishop informing him that we were all well; but no sooner had I done so than Gert Botha, who had been our right-hand man, suddenly became indisposed through drinking bad water. We were all much concerned about him, and so ill did he become, that we were obliged to put him to bed in the wagon, inspan at once, and trek for the camp in order to obtain medical assistance. On arrival there, Dr. Liknaitzky prescribed for him, and under his treatment, aided by the nursing of his bosom friend, Jacques de Toit, he soon recovered. Early the next morning, General Joubert, Mr. Melt Marais, and Colonel Ferreira arrived. The men of the Pretoria contingent spoke in high terms of the Colonel as an officer of ability, and his election as Commandant gave general satisfaction.

At the sound of the bugle all gathered around a wagon, upon which were a Dutch predikant from Pretoria, the General, Mr. Melt Marais, and Colonel Ferreira. A religious service was then held, and afterwards the General addressed the men. I could not understand what was said, as he spoke in Dutch, but it was evident that an impression was made, judging by the hearty cheers that were given at the end of the speech.

Although I did not leave my wagon, owing to the rain, I could hear all that passed, and was much impressed with the singing of the " Old Hundredth." It was raining during the whole of the proceedings.

'LARIDGE. GARTON. REMSAY. K. SHEPPARD HOLZER. W. KEITH.
STURMANN McMORLAND. HAUPT. LOVEDAY. B. YORKE-WATKINS.
(the "Boy.")

MESS No. 3.

[*To face page 17.*

CHAPTER III.

A DISORDERLY CAMP.

THE next day being Sunday, I held services in the camp for the first time both in the morning and evening. The singing was really good, and this was not to be wondered at, considering that four out of the twelve in my mess, and Lieutenant Holzer of mess No. 3, belonged to the cathedral choir.

At about noon, Messrs. Sonnenburg, Bartlett, and Jackson, from Pretoria, visited us and stayed to dinner. They brought with them sad news. On their way to the camp they met a transport rider named Van de Bijl, who asked them to come to his wagon. This they did, and were just in time to see Gert van de Westhuizen, one of the commandeered men, breathing his last. He had wandered from the commando to Van de Bijl, and asked him to give him a place to sleep in. Van de Bilj gave him permission to sleep under the wagon. It appeared that towards daylight, Van de Westhuizen walked to a tree about thirty yards away, and, after stabbing himself with his knife, staggered back to the wagon covered with blood. Upon being questioned by the astonished Van de Bijl, he replied that it was hard for him to leave his wife and family and be pressed into service, and that he wished to die. Lieutenant Schroeder, upon being informed of the sad occurrence, proceeded to the spot and had the body conveyed to the camp, where it awaited a medical examination. All the rest of the commando were well and in the best of spirits. During the afternoon, Dr. Tobias and Sergeant Charles Lever went out shooting, while Messrs. Holzer, Gates, Taylor, and Brook tried their skill at fishing; but both hunters and anglers were rewarded with very little sport. Corporal Gert Botha, still weak from the effects of his indisposition of the previous day, walked as far as the river, and venturing too near the edge of the bank, had the misfortune to slip in, but with no bad results, except, of course, a good wetting. Dr. Mader, the appointed medical officer to the commando, arrived, to whom I was introduced. He held a post-mortem on the body of poor Van de Westhuizen, and could form no opinion as to how the wounds were inflicted. The body was afterwards taken to Pretoria for burial. The deceased was a married man with a large family, and strongly protested against being commandeered. He left his family quite unprovided for.

The arrival of Colonel Ferreira was a matter of great rejoicing, for ever since the start there had not been the least order or discipline amongst the troops. Everyone did as he deemed fit, and the camp was in real danger, as shots were often fired at random. While at the Thorns, I saw one man, who was sitting on the voorkist of a wagon, level his gun and fire, and, when remonstrated with, said he was only testing his new rifle in order to be ready for Malaboch. Another brave soldier, who had never handled a Martini before, was in the act of demonstrating how he would shoot the enemy, when the gun exploded with a bang, and, with the recoil, the shooting-iron struck him on the nose. This caused much amusement, and the brave fellow, rubbing his nose and seeing the blood, quietly said, " I have drawn first blood. This is the blood of a warrior," and for a few days after he was the partaker of hospital comforts.

The Colonel soon enforced discipline, and I for one was relieved of much unnecessary anxiety. After the rambles of the day were over, and when everything was quiet, I held service at the Colonel's wagon. A huge fire was burning (for the night was cold), and this, with a few candle-lamps hung on the boughs of the trees, gave quite a brilliant light. By 10 P.M. all lights were out and everyone had retired.

CHAPTER IV.

A DAY'S HUNTING.

RÉVEILLE was sounded at 3 A.M., and at once the whole of the camp was astir. When the roll was called eighteen failed to respond, and the Colonel sent a telegram to this effect to headquarters. He (the Colonel) inspected the men in a business-like military fashion, and all were glad to have one in command who understood his work so thoroughly and was determined to do his duty at all hazards. There can be no doubt that, if the Colonel's ideas of organisation had been carried out as he wished, there would have been less confusion and discontent than unhappily prevailed afterwards to an alarming extent. By 5.30 the oxen were inspanned and we trekked for four hours, and encamped on the Pretoria side of the Pienaars River; but our stay here was very brief, for the General, who was on his way to Pietersburg by the coach, and whose arrival in camp was announced by vociferous cheering from the Boers, at once gave orders to trek on to the other side of the river, where we were to join the rest of the commando. The horsemen fell in for the first time under the command of Lieutenant Schroeder. They rode two and two, preceded by the

LIEUT. J. SCHROEDER,
Pretoria Horse.

[*To face page* 20.

Vierkleur, carried by Sergeant-Major Malan, who was accompanied by Bugler Sergeant Fuchs. The sight was very imposing, and great credit was due to the officer in charge for the able and efficient manner in which his onerous and thankless duties were performed. Had he, in conjunction with Colonel Ferreira, received that moral support from his superior officers—support to which he was certainly entitled, but instead of which was exposed to utter contumely —the history of the Pretoria contingent redounding to its credit, as it is, would have achieved still greater pre-eminence among its companion corps.

The wagons dragged along heavily, for it was still raining hard, which made everything wretched and miserable. We soon reached our new place of encampment, and for the first time were able to pitch a small tent and fix a bucksail to the side of the wagon; these had come with baggage-wagons that morning. They were a great boon and enabled us to sleep in comfort.

During the afternoon, a meeting of the committee of the hospital comforts was held in the Colonel's tent. The committee consisted of Dr. Mader, Colonel Ferreira, Dr. Tobias, Sergeant Charles Lever, and myself; Sergeant Charles Lever was appointed secretary, and, under the supervision of the committee, the wagon was unpacked and an inventory taken. These comforts consisted of all the necessaries of the Ambulance Corps. During our stay here we received a visit from the Chief Hans Makapan, who lived close by. He was attired in a smart mackintosh, a military peaked-cap, emblazoned with gold braid, and top-boots. He held an umbrella with red, white, blue, and yellow stripes, and was evidently well satisfied with himself. He conversed with the Colonel for some time and then apparently conferred with his indunas.

Austin Brook was told off with others for horse guard, much to his disgust, as it was still raining very hard; after his spell of duty, he crept into the wagon wet through. The next morning, after breakfast, I went out hunting with Mauritz Preller. We walked for miles through the long wet grass, and although I had my top-boots on, my feet got very wet. We were not very fortunate, for though we saw several koraan we failed to bag them; Mauritz, however, shot a solitary guinea-fowl out of a large drove. Dr. Tobias, who had gone in another direction, had better sport, and brought back four brace of plump partridge. We returned for luncheon, and afterwards Dr. Tobias accompanied us on another hunt: this time we were on horseback. Lovell Taylor was good enough to lend me his shot-gun and well-filled bandolier; but although we saw numbers of guinea-fowl, our luck was no better than that of the morning. The doctor had brought his dog (a brown pointer), and when he potted the only bird of the afternoon, the dog had been lost, so was not there to assist in the search, and consequently, the grass being very long, we had to return without it. Reaching the wagons, which were still advancing, I again started out with Lieutenant Eloff and another, buck-

THE PRETORIA HORSE IN FRONT OF BLAAUWBERG.

hunting this time, ultimately returning still empty handed. I then joined my mess, feeling much disgusted and very tired. Our poor oxen were so weak that they were unable to proceed with the others, and we had to outspan some distance from the camp. We spent another very wretched night, for, owing to the incessant downpour, we were unable to pitch a tent, and were obliged to retire in the wagon. I had no sleep the whole night through, and my back ached so much that I felt quite sick, and was very glad when daylight appeared.

CHAPTER V.

THE WARM BATHS.

AFTER the night's rest, our bullocks, although no better fit than they were the previous day, were obliged to be inspanned, and Gert Botha (Gerard) allowed them practically to make their own time, for fear of knocking them up altogether. I am afraid we could never have caught up to the main column had not Colonel Ferreira, who passed us on his way to the camp, sent us six fresh bullocks. It was a great relief to be able to keep going at a reasonable speed, for even at the best of times bullock travelling is, to say the least of it, slow and monotonous.

On joining our comrades of the main column, I left on horseback, with Sergeant Charles Lever, for the purpose of visiting the warm baths, situated in the Waterberg District. On our way thither we saw several buck, and Charles managed to bring down a steinbok. He dismounted, and putting down his gun proceeded to search for the buck. The horse at once bolted, making straight for a field of amabele at some distance off. I followed on horseback, leaving my companion still engaged in the search. Having captured the runaway I returned to assist Charles to find the buck. We found it and secured it to the saddle. We had now forgotten where the gun was laid, which necessitated another search, and we were much hampered therein by the long grass. However, all's well that ends well, and gun, buck, and horse were eventually secured.

We then resumed our journey, when we met a Kafir girl, of whom we asked the way; but, instead of replying, she cleared off as fast as she could, probably terrified by our warlike appearance. On reaching the Warm Baths Hotel, we found Lieutenant Schroeder, with about forty horsemen, already there, and we all dined together.

I am told that the medicinal properties of these hot springs are similiar to those of Baden Baden.

Tony Vlotman, who had also bagged a buck, returned with us to the camp immediately after dinner. That evening I supped with the Colonel, and retired very early.

A parade and kit inspection was held early the next morning by Commandant Erasmus and the Colonel; when the roll was called, seven were still missing. The appointment of the officers were now confirmed. The Commandant complimented the men on their smart appearance, adding that he felt sure they would do their duty for "Land en Volk." Lieutenant Schroeder kept his men well under control, and made the slow ones "brush up," and I consider the compliment well deserved. After three cheers had been given, we trekked on to Tweefontein, still in the Waterberg District. Grumbling occurred at times, and a little strong language was indulged in; but then the weather was very wet, and the organisation decidedly bad, as no rations had yet been served out, and this was the ninth day en route. Some suffered from actual want in consequence.

On leaving Tweefontein, the roads became very heavy; our oxen stuck several times, and everyone had literally to put his shoulder to the wheel, as the wagons had sunk in the deep sand. As we passed through the bush-veld, care had also to be taken, because of the overhanging boughs. Tons of rough wood were lying about, and this no doubt was secured by the burghers on their return. A little incident occurred here, which caused some excitement and amusement. A supposed steinbok ran across the road, and many jumped off the wagons and gave chase; the Colonel's two greyhounds joined in the chase, but they were not at all keen on it. After all, the supposed buck turned out to be a jackal.

We outspanned at a pretty little spot between Buiskop and Krantz Kop.

We trekked early the next morning, and outspanned at Krantz Kop. There was not quite so much bush here as at our last outspan. After breakfasting with the Colonel, I went to look at the river we had just crossed, more out of curiosity than anything else, as I had been told that it was the River Nile. I was most anxious to see this ancient river, but I have since discovered that this name had its origin from the fact, that the geographers of two and half centuries ago held a fixed idea that the sources of the Nile were somewhere in Southern

Africa. Many of the old trekkers still clung to this belief; and in 1875, a section of the Doppers (who consider themselves a chosen people, having for an inheritance the heathen, whom they regard as fit only to be slaves), with their wives and families and all their belongings, trekked to Mossamedes, expecting to find the Nijl, as they spelt it, somewhere in the north or north-west of the Transvaal, where they would find rich pastures abounding in game. Hence the present name of the river and town of Nijl-stroom, in the Waterberg District. After resting here for a short time, we made a very long trek, lasting nearly five hours. The roads were still very heavy, and the oxen almost worn out. We at last reached Badzijnloop. I at once left with Gerard to try and shoot partridge; but, after walking some miles, we returned without having seen a bird or fired a shot. There was a post office here, and we were able to send off our mail.

CHAPTER VI.

A DESERTER

At daybreak we were off again, and trekked till 5.30 A.M. As soon as we had outspanned, the Colonel's two dogs barked and scampered off in pursuit of a poor little rabbit, which had ventured into the camp; but it got away, and the dogs were soon back, and I came to the conclusion that they were as good at hunting as myself, and that was not saying much.

The nights and mornings were cold, and this morning the ground was covered with a thick hoar frost.

A supply of guns and ammunition having arrived at Pietersburg, Messrs. Vlotman and Brook received instructions to proceed thither.

We rested the next day, it being Sunday, although all, from the Commandant downwards, were anxious to reach the seat of war with the least possible delay; yet we dared not travel on the "Sabbath," for that would be desecration, and reverses would be sure to follow, such is the general belief amongst the Boers; also we should run the risk of being mulcted in a heavy fine for breaking the laws of the land; so we rested. I held service at 10 A.M., after which the

OFFICERS AND NON-COMMISSIONED OFFICERS OF THE PRETORIA TOWN CONTINGENT.

[*To face page* 29.

Colonel ordered a parade, and on the roll being called, every man answered to his name.

Dick Amos, the camp tailor, was busy the whole day with his needle, sewing on stripes to the officers' uniforms, which were thus decorated for the first time. The Colonel, who had gone to Nijlstroom with the mail, returned, bringing back with him a deserter, who had stolen a horse, saddle, bridle, and two oxen, and had disposed of the latter for fifteen shillings the two. The Colonel sent for four Englishmen of the navvy type, all of them old soldiers, having done short service under the Queen's colours, to guard the prisoner, who, having received their charge, secured the poor wretch by passing a rope loosely round his neck, the two ends of it being held by the guard (*nota bene*, "it" is the rope, not the neck). Thus, had the prisoner attempted to make a dash for liberty, he would have been strangled. No doubt the guard were somewhat terrified by the Colonel's remarks, who, assuming a stern attitude, said : "I have picked out you, whom I consider the four best men in the commando, and if you dare to let the prisoner escape, you will be dead men by daylight." He (the prisoner) was brought to the Colonel's wagon and guarded in the manner described, and standing with his guard close to a huge log fire (my only light for the evening service) he looked an object of pity, and my thoughts were much distracted during the service by his dejected appearance. I felt inclined to speak to the man, but restrained from so doing out of regard for military discipline.

Dr. Tobias, who ranked as sergeant and acted as postmaster, had also the onerous duties of giving out each day's orders; and his bright and happy manner of doing so often evoked a laugh from the men, and onlookers from other contingents, for it was only in Colonel Ferreira's contingent that strict military discipline was observed. After instructing the men as to their duties for the following day, he would announce that a religious service would be held for the benefit of the deep-dyed blackguards whom he was then addressing, and he hoped that they would all attend, and amend their wicked ways. Instructions were also given at this period as to the rations each burgher was to receive. The genial doctor stated that each man would be served out per diem with 2 lbs. meat, 1 oz. coffee, 2 oz. sugar, 2 beekers of meal ($1\frac{1}{2}$ lbs.), and 10 beekers of mealies for each horse. We had now been on the road twelve days and had received no regular food, although we had been told at the start that on and after the eighth day rations would be supplied regularly. However, the majority had made ample provision, and, thanks to the kind forethought of Pretoria friends, Mrs. Burnham's box now came into requisition, and it would be difficult to describe the joy the opening of it gave us. Before retiring I took a stroll round the camp, accompanied by Jacques du Toit and Lovell Taylor. Fires were burning at every wagon, and the Boers were singing the Old Hundredth, every man, apparently, trying to outdo the other in slowness of time, each note being prolonged for at least six beats.

Our next outspan was at Naboomfontein, where we stayed a few hours. While our boy was inspanning, one of the after oxen kicked him, sending him flying. Everyone this morning seemed to be in a gloomy mood, and a cantankerous spirit was prevalent, due probably to the fact of being called up at 2 A.M. The younger men who at first were so anxious to go as substitutes, now knew, to their cost, that going to fight Malaboch was not such a pleasant picnic as they had anticipated, and many of them wished themselves back under the parental roof. One of our Kafirs met with a very serious accident; the wheel of the wagon going over his leg, just above the ankle, completely severing the sinews and tendons.

Dr. Mader, who was soon on the spot, dressed the wound and stitched it up; during this operation the poor " boy " groaned with pain. He would never, the doctor said, have the proper use of his foot again, but would have to walk on his toes; some friends of his from a kraal close by came and took him away. We proceeded and outspanned near Moord Drift. The Colonel left us here and went with his prisoner to Pietpotgieters Rust. The guard were glad enough to be relieved of their responsibility. A hare which ran through the camp was bowled over by a Kafir, with a chopper.

Our next trek was the longest we ever did, viz. eight hours, all but five minutes; it was necessary for us to make so long an inspan in order to reach water at Biltong-fontein.

Here bad news was brought us by Sergeant-Major Malan, to the effect that Malaboch's men had come out of their stronghold and had attacked our troops, driving them back several times. A patrol, while digging sweet potatoes in a kraal, was fired on. The report of arms caused two of their horses to bolt, and one of the dismounted men received a flesh wound in the head; another, an Englishman, was wounded in the chest, and a Boer had his hat shot off.

CHAPTER VII.

A NOCTURNAL FLITTING—THE MALABOCH WAR SONG.

THE following day we heard, by a Kafir runner, that General Joubert had been bitten behind the ear by a poisonous spider: his condition was reported as serious, and Dr. Mader at once proceeded with an escort to attend him.

The trek to-day was continued through very beautiful scenery, and we passed a few homesteads on our way. I walked up a small kopje with several companions and saw a number of salamanders (a species of lizard). On our return to the camp Mauritz Preller and Durbin Brice were tried by court-martial for refusing to go on sentry duty the previous night. The verdict was, that in addition to their usual duty, they were to do extra horse-guard as a punishment for their insubordination. There was still a little grumbling going on amongst a few of the Pretoria men, because of the discipline which was being rigidly enforced. Petitions from the grumblers were signed and handed in to the Commandant, who, to his credit, refused to interfere, knowing full well how absolutely necessary strict order and discipline are to ensure the safety of an invading force, especially when almost face to face with the enemy. The startling news of the morning made the Colonel extra cautious, and while the wagons were *en route* a guard of four men to each was put on, one on either side of the voorlooper, and two bringing up the rear. After travelling in this way for nearly three hours, we caught a first glimpse of the enemy's mountain, and this was our landmark for the rest of the journey. By the time we outspanned, the apprehension caused by the morning's news had subsided, and during their idle time the men amused themselves by " throwing the oxhide," a most foolish and dangerous pastime, practised by the Boers. An oxhide is procured and held by about twelve men; an unfortunate bystander is placed in the middle of the hide, and at a given signal jerked up in the air by the twelve, who catch him in his descent; some were thrown up a tremendous height and fell all of a heap, and it is a marvel to me no bones were broken. Durbin Brice, who was thrown much against his will, ricked his neck, and felt the effects for some days. This idiotic practice seemed to gratify the childish minds of our Boer friends, until the Commandant forbade it under penalty of a heavy fine.

During the outspan—the first after catching sight of the enemy's hills—the men were paraded before Commandant Erasmus, who, through Corporal Frans Conradie acting as interpreter, read out certain camp regulations, having special reference to the extinguishing of lights, and the conduct of the men generally, in the prospective presence of the enemy, and he expressed a hope that these regulations would not be infringed.

The evening was cold, and we gathered round the wagon of Dr. Tobias and held an *al fresco* concert. The doctor sang for the first time the "Malaboch War Song" of his own composition, all joining in the chorus vigorously, betokening that their sorrow of the morning was but skin-deep. By 9 P.M. all lights were out, and silence reigned in camp; this was as it should be, considering the enemy's close proximity.

This being my first experience of a war expedition, these restrictions naturally caused me some little uneasiness, and I was not alone in my fears. I had retired in the wagon by the side of Gerard, and had fallen asleep, when I was suddenly awakened about midnight, by feeling the rugs roughly pulled off me, and starting up to ascertain the cause, found my companion had decamped with all the bedding through the back of the wagon. I shouted out, "Gerard, where are you going?" but receiving no reply, I bounded nimbly through the front, and stood with bare feet on the veld in bewilderment. I quite thought the enemy was upon us, and had hauled Gerard out to assegai him, but everything being perfectly still, I ventured round to the back of the wagon, and found my friend "not" full of assegais, but scratching his head and rubbing his leg, for he had come into violent contact with the handle of the brakescrew, and had it not been for the bedclothes, the consequences would have been much more serious No Kafirs were there, and on my asking

Gerard the why and wherefore of this nocturnal flitting, and whether he was hurt, he replied, "I'm not hurt, I was only dreaming." Frans Conradie, who was sleeping under the wagon, and who was also disturbed by this commotion, simply roared with laughter at our conversation.

We climbed back again into the wagon, and Gerard related his dream as follows:—"I dreamt that I was in my house in Pretoria, looking out of the front window, when I saw Mauritz passing on a restive horse which threw him; his foot caught in the stirrup and he was being dragged along the road. I heard him crying out for help, and opening the window, I jumped out to stop the horse which was going at full galop." Jacques, who had been on guard, turned in soon after this little escapade, frozen with cold, but we were so excited that we got little or no sleep that night.

MALABOCH WAR SONG.

Composed by the late Dr. F. B. TOBIAS.

Arranged by T. H. FARRAR.

Ons gaat ten oor-log, Mal-a-boch! Mal-a-boch! Ons gaat jou haal, Je moet op-betaal, Ons zal jou skiet op com-mando van Oom Piet.

2.

Hou jou maar klaar,
      Malaboch! Malaboch!
Ons heb't Zwaar
Dat is waarachtig waar
Ons krijg jou toch
Jou vervloekste Malaboch.

(Chorus.)

3.

God die alles weet,
      Malaboch! Malaboch!
Zorg voor vrouw en kind
Broeders, zusters, en vriend
Liefjes die ons laat
Kan niet schelen hoe't gaat.

(Chorus.)

4.

Ons Kornel Ferreira,
      Malaboch! Malaboch!
Komt met zijn perden
Om jou te keeren
Ons gaat te voet
En ons slaat jou op jou snoet.

(Chorus.)

5.

Ons Reverend Colin Rae,
      Malaboch! Malaboch!
Met hom is ons te vrij
Hij gaat overal mee
Waar blijft die predikant
Van ons dierbaar Vaderland.

(Chorus.)

6.

Ons Commandant Generaal,
    Malaboch! Malaboch!
Hou niet van dit geschiet
Neuk maar met de dynamiet
Hij heeft jou amper gefop
Met de klippers op jou kop.

(Chorus.)

7.

Neen, zeg Commandant Malan,
    Malaboch! Malaboch!
Ons het een ander plan
Wat jou nie vatte kan
Kan je dit niet zien
Ons moet rook met paraffin.

(Chorus.)

8.

Ons was ten oorlog,
    Malaboch! Malaboch!
Ons't jou gehaal
Je't op betaal
Ons't jou geschiet
Op Commando van Oom Piet.

(Chorus.)

(*English translation by* EDYTHE E. TOWNSEND.)

1.

We're coming to war!
   Malaboch! Malaboch!
For your sins you must pay,
Uncle Piet bids us "slay"!
Get ready for the strife,
You must fight for your life.

(*Chorus.*)

And so long as the spoon in the porridge pot stands,
 We will never mourn,
Nor will we complain;
And so long as the spoon in the porridge pot stands,
 We will never mourn.

2.

Hold yourself ready!
   Malaboch! Malaboch!
Though rough and long the way,
We will not halt nor stay—
For thy black blood we thirst,
Thou Malaboch *accurst!*

(*Chorus.*)

3.

God above knows all—
   Malaboch! Malaboch!
He'll hear our fervent call
And grant no harm befall
Mother, child, and wife—
Loved ones, dearer than life.

(*Chorus.*)

4.

Our Brave Ferreira!
   Malaboch! Malaboch!
With his fleet and prancing steeds
Will soon stop your evil deeds,
And though we on foot must go
We can deal a killing blow.

 (*Chorus.*)

5.

The Reverend Colin Rae,
   Malaboch! Malaboch!
Our devoted friend
Goes with us to thine end,
But where is the priest
Of our belov'd Fatherland?

 (*Chorus.*)

6.

Our Commandant General—
   Malaboch! Malaboch!
He could shoot you at sight
But prefers dynamite!
You may well go in dread,
With the stones thrown at your head.

 (*Chorus.*)

7.

No! said Commandant Malan,
   Malaboch! Malaboch!
A game I have planned
Which you cannot understand;
But you'll see what I mean
When we smoke with paraffin!

 (*Chorus.*)

8.

We've been to the war,
    Malaboch! Malaboch!
A captive you are made
And the price you have paid ;
Sad and sore your defeat—
Three cheers for Uncle Piet!

(*Chorus.*)

N.B. This is a free translation. Were the literal English produced, I fear that most of my readers would find such almost unintelligible.—*The Author.*

CHAPTER VIII.

THE REVEREND MR. PARISIUS.

WE were off again the next morning at 6.50, and had to foot it, owing to the bad state of the roads. Gerard alone remained in the wagon, as he could scarcely stir, through the effects of his bruises. We reached Mathala's kraal about four hours later, in bitterly cold weather. I called on the Rev. Mr. Parisius, the German Lutheran missionary, who received me most kindly and offered me breakfast. This station is prettily situated under the shelter of a huge kopje. The house is approached by a very pretty avenue of the poisonous Euphorbia; the garden was well stocked with orange-trees, which were laden with delicious fruit, and I was invited to help myself.

The Chief Mathala came out to meet the Colonel and held a long conversation with him. He (the Chief) wished to know where the Colonel had got the Kafir corn from, which he saw in the wagon. He was most impudent, and said we had no right to steal the corn from his lands, and that we should not have outspanned where we did the previous night. After this confab, he informed the Colonel that Malaboch had three impis out, but he estimated their full strength at about a thousand, and consequently thought that a few hours' fighting would settle the whole matter, or, as he expressed himself, " you will make a breakfast off Malaboch." Malaboch, he said, had driven off his cattle to Bamangwato; he (Mathala) had already sent 500 of his men to the front.

After this interview he presented the Colonel with a magnificent pig and five oxen. The pig, he said, was the one his father had promised the Colonel in 1876; it was certainly very fat, and Mr. Piet Louw, the camp butcher, estimated its weight at 600 lbs., but this was not to be wondered at, considering that it had taken eighteen years (?) to fatten.

Messrs. Vlotman and Brook returned from Pietersburg with the arms and ammunition at this time, and their arrival was greeted with acclamation. A better spirit prevailed than hitherto. Colonel Ferreira, in consequence of the continued dissatisfaction of certain chronic grumblers, who refused to obey orders, and thus kicked against the discipline he had introduced, threatened to resign his position as Commandant, and proceed to the front merely as a private individual, rendering what assistance he could. He informed Commandant Erasmus to this effect, who, not only refused to accept his resignation, but gave him entire control over his own troops, even to the drafting of his own camp rules. This proved satisfactory to everybody concerned, save to the few already referred to, whose only reason for disregarding orders was that they might get out of horse-guard and sentry duties. During Mathala's interview, arrangements were made for a regular postal service by means of Kafir-runners to and from Pietersburg and the seat of war.

The next outspan brought us to Tubaan's Loop, Mathala and the Rev. Mr. Parisius accompanying us on horseback; before they left, the pig was killed and quartered. What with pork, curry, rice, and potatoes, the latter brought with the ordnance from Pietersburg, we had a most sumptuous repast, the enjoyment of which was enhanced by the music of a guitar artistically fingered by our popular mess-mate, Gert Botha. The success of this meal, the best we had had since leaving Pretoria, was entirely due to the skill of Sergeant Tony Vlotman, an old "bush-craftsman," who was well experienced in the art of open-air cookery. After dinner we sang songs round the camp-fire, and had quite a large audience, which joined heartily in the choruses. The war song was the favourite, and had already become very popular both amongst the Burghers and Uitlanders.

"Good old Tob," as Dr. Tobias was called, not only sang the song, but put in much "business," causing roars of laughter, and I am quite certain the doctor thought that the song could not be rendered effectively except by himself, and I quite agreed with him.

The next morning I witnessed an interesting sight. The women from kraals near by, which were hidden by a perfect maze of prickly pear bushes, came to the wagons bearing on their heads baskets containing mealies, pumpkins, beans, sweet potatoes, amabele, eggs, and fowls. All these were bartered for beef and "tickeys." This bartering lasted the whole day and part of the next. Pickets were stationed all over the place, on the hills, and both inside and outside the camp. Watkins, of wagon number three, was doing picket duty on the top of a huge rock; he was shivering with cold, and was glad enough when he received instructions to descend. All this picketing was the result of groundless fears, as the enemy would not dare to venture into the territory of Marthala, he being a much more powerful chief than Malaboch, and at enmity with him.

We received instructions to wait here for reinforcements from Rustenburg, which were expected in a few days.

The next day I secured a mount from Lieutenant Schroeder, and went in company with Mr. F. Neel, Assistant-Surgeon, and Mr. Kaiser, the War Secretary, on a visit to the Rev. Mr. Parisius, a distance of about nine miles. We found the reverend gentleman riding round his lands, who, on seeing us, invited us to his house, where his devoted and genial wife regaled us with coffee and cakes.

A missionary's life is not, as some people imagine, one of ease and plenty, but, on the contrary, is, in my opinion, one of the hardest and most trying means of existence. The solitariness of such a life is one of the greatest trials. Mr. Parisius, who had been stationed at this mission for nine years, informed me that, during that time, he had sometimes gone for nearly a year without ever seeing a white stranger; and I know from experience that if it were not for assistance from Europe, the missionary would fare very badly, for the Kafir very rarely has money to offer, and when he has it, is so fascinated with it, that he miserly hoards it up. Our kind host and hostess hastened to prepare luncheon for us, which consisted of boiled fowl, potatoes, and sauer-kraut. After this repast we bade our friends adieu, and hurried back to camp, reaching there just before dark.

The expected Rustenburgers arrived in due course, and on their advent the serious part of the campaign commenced, and the picnic part ceased.

CHAPTER IX.

AN INTERESTING DAY.

By this time my hair had grown uncomfortably thick and long, and while returning from the mission station, my friend, Neel, promised to cut it for me, so, as soon as we returned to camp, he lost no time in commencing the operation; but, unfortunately, darkness set in before he had finished, and he coolly informed me that he would complete the job in the morning, so I had to retire with my head half shorn. I was up betimes in the morning, and roused Neel at eight o'clock, when he soon finished his task in a very creditable way.

This day (Sunday) was one of much interest. First of all I held a service for the Pretoria contingent at 10.30 A.M., and afterwards visited the kraal with Mauritz Preller, Lovell Taylor, and Austin Brook; several curios were secured here, including an old blunderbuss, which Mauritz bought for nine shillings and sixpence. Later on, Jacques de Toit came, and was curious enough to taste a roasted locust. He said the flavour was very salt, something like a shrimp. The natives were having their dinner off locusts and mealie pap. They were very hospitable, and invited me to partake of what they

E

had; but though I accepted some mealie pap to avoid giving offence, I had not the courage to crunch up a locust.

At 4.30 in the afternoon I held a service for the Dutch. Vested in cassock, surplice, and stole, I walked to the tent of Commandant Erasmus, who had made every preparation; a dais, consisting of old boxes, had been erected in the open air, behind which were placed two chairs, one for Frans Conradie, who kindly acted as interpreter, and the other for myself. It was a simple service, as follows:—A hymn (in Dutch), prayer (in English), a chapter of the Scriptures (in Dutch) by Mr. Frans Conradie, another hymn (in Dutch), sermon interpreted, and a closing hymn (in Dutch). I preached from the text, "The battle is the Lord's," and about four hundred men listened to the sermon in profound silence. My Dutch consisted of the Invocation before the sermon, "In den naam van den Vader, en van den Zoon, en van den Heiligen Geest, Amen," and at the close of the service, 2 Corinthians xiii. 14: "De genad van ons Heere Jesus Christus, en de liefde van God, en de gemeenschap des Heiligen Geest zij met u all voor eenwig, Amen."

After I had returned to my wagon the Commandant came and thanked me on behalf of the burghers and himself for the words I had spoken, and expressed a hope that the service would be often repeated; at the same time he complimented Mr. Frans Conradie for his accurate interpretation. I felt grateful to hear this, knowing, as I do, the attitude of a Boer to an

PRETORIA TOWN PATROLS. [*To face page* 51.

MAMATOLLA

Uitlander, especially an Englishman, who cannot speak his language.

We finished up the day with an English service, held round the Colonel's fire, and retired early, as we had to resume the march betimes the next morning. Our stay here had lasted three days. In the morning, Gerard shot his fourteenth ox, which was served out as rations. The whole of the fourteen had been killed by that number of bullets, he never having missed his aim.

The roll was again called, and instructions were given for everyone to be ready for trekking at noon. I walked up a kopje near by with Charles Lever, and had an awkward climb; while going through one of the kloofs a young owl flew past us, and, in a dark cave, into which we peered, we saw, by the aid of a lighted match, a fierce old owl, whose eyes seemed to pierce us through, but we thought it prudent to leave it alone, and did. It was evident that this kopje had been used at some time or other as a Kafir stronghold, there being old ruins of forts and schantzes round about. When we reached the camp again we saw Mamatolla, an old local chieftainess, with some of her followers, mostly women, squatting round the Colonel's tent. He (the Colonel) treated her to a substantial breakfast of about two pounds of beef, and some biscuits, which she devoured ravenously, all by herself, and then asked for more (which she didn't get).

Mr. F. Neel sketched her on the spot, which is here reproduced. Mr. Zeederberg, from Pietersburg, arrived in a wagonette drawn by four mules, and left again for Blaauwberg in advance of the commando.

We trekked again at 12.15 P.M. Flanking parties were thrown out, and the train of wagons was protected by front and rear-guards. For the last two nights many fires had been observed at some distance from the camp, extending over an area of many miles. From these indications we judged that information was being conveyed to Malaboch concerning our movements. The previous night a large veld-fire was distinctly seen in the route we had to take, and it was supposed that the Kafirs were burning the grass in front of us to prevent our oxen getting anything to eat. Several of our men were suffering from fever and dysentery, which maladies were ascribed to the brackish water we had to drink while encamped at Tubaan. A report reached us that the General's condition was still critical, no improvement being perceptible. As we trekked steadily along, all who were not on guard were seated in the wagon; and Austin Brook, Jacques du Toit, and myself read aloud in turn "Silver Domino," which had been lent me by Lieutenant Rice.

There were millions and millions of locusts in and around our camp. After partaking of some of Tony Vlotman's Irish stew, for which he had now got quite a name, we started again. All the footmen of my mess walked alongside the wagon armed. A message reached us from the General to the effect that two hundred of the cavalry were to leave the main body and proceed by forced marches to the seat of war. The messenger informed us that Malaboch had sent to the General, by his (Malaboch's) brother, a white ox and twenty pounds. Upon the General asking the meaning of it all, the answer was, that the white ox was a token of peace, and the twenty pounds a suitable present to the white chief. The General replied, "If Malaboch wants peace he must come down from the mountain with all his men and I will give him a place to live in on the flat." The messenger said, "Malaboch is afraid that if he came down he and his people would starve, as all the corn had been captured or burned." The General answered, "If Malaboch obeys, I will find him corn for himself and people; I will give him until Monday to submit: if he refuses he must take the consequences." It was the general impression that there was a compact amongst the tribes, with the Chief Magato at their head, to resist, and that all this talk was to gain time. This, however, fitted in with the General's arrangements, as it enabled him to mobilise his forces. All Malaboch's Kafirs had left their locations and had gone on to the mountain. It was the opinion that Malaboch would soon surrender. The camp was thrown into great excitement at this warlike news.

I should have mentioned that after leaving the mission station orders were given for all firing of guns to cease; up till now everybody had been banging away at random, without the least restriction. Two burghers soon infringed this rule. After leaving Tubaan, seeing some buck on the veld, the temptation was so great, as they explained when being tried by Commandant Erasmus, that they could not resist firing at them. No doubt in passing sentence the Commandant took this fact into consideration, as they were only fined five shillings each (the full penalty being £10), and then one of them had to borrow a shilling to make up the required sum. The man was of fine physique, and had a good-natured face, and both he and his companion were much frightened, and seemed to think that this act of disobedience simply meant decapitation.

CHAPTER X.

THE FIRST SKIRMISH.

OUR next two treks brought us to the base of operations. We arrived there at 2 P.M., June 12th, having been on the road twenty-one days from Pretoria. These two last treks covered a distance of about twenty-five miles, and we passed through dense swarms of locusts; in fact, it may be well described as twenty-five miles of locust-infested veld. There was a rumour current that we were to make an attack that same evening. It was evident, however, that all did not take this information seriously, Mr. Austin Brook in particular, for he continued reading " Silver Domino " to his comrades, and was totally ignorant of the fact that he would really face the enemy the next day.

A parade was called soon after our arrival, and the genial doctor gave out the orders in his usual happy, light-hearted way, telling all the men to be in readiness for an attack at 3 A.M. Before retiring I accompanied Mr. Kaiser on a visit to the Commandant-General, who was still confined to his bed. After a formal introduction by Mr. Kaiser, His Honour asked me if I could speak in Dutch, and on my replying in the negative, he conversed with me freely in English.

I did not, however, ask any questions as to future war operations, but merely condoled with him in his misfortune, and after expressing a wish for his speedy recovery, I returned to my tent. The expected attack did not come off the next morning; but between 9 and 10 A.M., the Colonel, Mr. Zeederberg, Lieutenant Eloff, Sergeant-Major Malan, and Mr. Kling (who acted as cook to the Colonel) proceeded to the mountain, and set fire to twenty-two huts. We saw them burning from the laager. On their return, the Colonel informed me that the enemy had fired twice upon them, which was not returned. He, however, organised an expedition for the afternoon, when about two hundred of the cavalry and twenty-eight infantry reconnoitred the mountain.

Austin Brook, of the infantry, related to me the following :—

"As soon as we had set fire to some huts, the enemy opened a heavy fire on us—I should think about forty rounds—but without effect. We held our position until a shot came from our rear. Thinking the enemy had surrounded us, we thought it prudent to retire, and on doing so, found that the shot had been fired by the guard left in charge of the horses at the foot of the hill. As we were retreating, between twenty and thirty of the enemy tried to cut us off by attacking us on our left flank, a movement which might have been successfully carried out had they exercised a little skill, as we only numbered twenty-eight, all the cavalry having left us on reaching the foot of the hill. Fortunately, their guns were of the old muzzle-loader type, and, consequently, their bark was worse than their bite. We are all here safely, as you see, and quite ready for dinner. Have you got any?"

Needless to say we had, and we all sat down together once more with forebodings as to whether it would be the last time we should enjoy that pleasure *en masse*.

When the cavalry returned, some time after dark, they were almost frantic with excitement, and proved that the majority of them were novices at soldiering, although an occasional old warrior could be easily detected. Many were the tales of hair-breadth escapes told round the camp-fires that night.

Whatever their experiences may have been, it put the funks into some of them, from which they never recovered until the day they started for home. "Feather-bed soldiers" some of them were, and no mistake.

Before retiring, orders were received from Commandant Erasmus for all the cavalry, and twenty of the infantry, to be in readiness for an attack early the next morning. This arrangement was altogether contrary to the Colonel's wishes, who had quite another plan, and he was much disgusted at not being consulted. It was very late when we retired, as we were too excited to sleep, and could only discuss the probable movements of the next day.

I spent a very restless night. Firing from other contingents was going on all through the night. The Commandant's plan, after all, was not put into effect, for at 1.30, every man, except about twenty, who were left to guard the camp, was up and armed with his rifle and revolver, the General having decided to make a determined attack from both sides of the mountain with all available forces. The Pretorians were to attack from the south-west of the berg, the Waterbergers from the opposite side, while the artillery brought a seven-pounder and a small mountain gun into play, the latter being taken right up the berg, the idea being to seize the second kopje in the range, which was some six miles away from the enemy's stronghold, and so gain a foothold on the mountain from which to conduct future operations. There were in our column alone, which included the Zoutpansberg men, about three hundred horsemen, a large contingent of footmen, two hundred friendly natives, and one gun.

Accordingly, at three o'clock, each Veld-Cornet and Commandant of divisions received orders to advance his men to the attack, an order which they proceeded to execute in the most ridiculous manner imaginable. There was neither order nor method about the whole thing, but it was simply a farce throughout, and resulted in a few doing the work, while the majority lay down in small parties before they had advanced two hundred yards.

Fortunately, the enemy offered very little opposition. They only fired a few straggling shots, and then slipped stealthily away, so stealthily as to be almost unnoticeable; in fact, one of the Pietersburg men (T. H. McArthur), who was amongst the

TROOPER T. H. McARTHUR,
Zoutpansberg Contingent.

first to meet the fire, remarked, "I did not see more than half a score of them during the whole morning's engagement."

A stad belonging to Malaboch's brother was burned, the occupants having left just previous to our arrival.

On reaching the summit, the mountain gun was placed in position, and operations were commenced on the surrounding bush, where it was thought the enemy might be concealed.

The combined forces, having mustered on the top of the berg, they immediately commenced to build a fort, a task soon accomplished, there being plenty of loose stones lying about.

Forty men, chosen from the Pretoria and Zoutpansberg contingents, were then left to man it, until the Waterburgers returned to take possession. This position was a most important one, and proved to be the key of the whole berg.

The only casualty of the day happened to a young fellow named George, who received a slight wound in the neck, and the incident proved to be of a most laughable nature.

The men had met at the fort, when a loud report was heard, and on everyone seizing his rifle, preparing to return the fire (as they thought), George was seen dancing about like a fanatic, holding both hands to his neck, and shouting out, "I have got it!" Everyone thought he had been shot, some asserting that it was a revolver bullet, but on Mr. Snyman, of Pietersburg, examining the wound, he found it to have been caused by the explosion of a detonator from a shell. How it came there nobody knew, but it was that that caused Mr. George to have " got it."

Great dissatisfaction prevailed in camp at the absurdly inadequate supply of provisions and clothing; wagons had arrived, bringing with them one bag of coffee, four bags of meal, four boxes of candles, six pairs of kharki trousers, and four Kafir blankets. These were for the supply of the whole laager. We had had no sugar issued for over a fortnight, only four pockets (weighing about seventy-five pounds each) having been loaded in Pretoria for the use of six hundred men. At that time a number of men were without blankets, boots, and other necessaries; several were literally walking about in rags. One man, who had badly torn his clothes while climbing the hill the previous day, had to borrow a mackintosh from one of his comrades, in order to hide his rags and to appear on parade. In this garment he performed his daily duties. Mr. Piet Zeederberg left the camp for the purpose of purchasing supplies, but it was an almost indisputable fact that in the whole of the Zoutpansberg district not more than one hundred bags of meal could be obtained. The urgency of the situation could not have been too strongly impressed upon the Government, as any addition to the great dissatisfaction then prevailing could only have led to the most disastrous results.

Commandant Pretorius, who had been for five days on a most successful patrol, proved, by the numbers of cattle he had captured, that the information given with regard to Malaboch's attempt to send his cattle over the border was correct.

Kiviet and Mapen, two friendly Chiefs, were assisting us by harassing Malaboch on the other side of the mountain.

During the advance of the Waterberg commando a young Kafir girl was unfortunately shot. She had received no less than three bullets. The mistake was quite unavoidable, owing to the blackness and density of the bush.

Whilst occupied in building a fort for the reception of one of the six-pounders, a man was severely bitten in two places by a scorpion, but receiving immediate treatment from Dr. Mader there were no serious results.

The General was now said to be quite convalescent. The health of the camp continued good, but owing to the insufficient supply of vegetables, there were several cases of veld sores.

After the fighting was over the bodies of more than thirty natives were found, but these were supposed to represent but one-third of the enemy's loss. At one of the captured schantzes Austin, Mauritz, and Gerard drew my attention to the mark of one of our bullets which was within two inches of one of the loop-holes. The shooting of the natives, so far as direction went, had been good; but they did not seem to understand elevation, and judging by the sound of their bullets, their ammunition was of very inferior quality. Had the positions we had taken been defended by a score of determined men, there was not the slightest doubt that we could never have obtained a footing. Numerous schantzes had been thrown up in places commanding the whole hill, and another splendid cover was afforded by the bush and rocks, which cover was fully taken advantage of by the invading forces as they gradually approached the stronghold.

CHAPTER XI.

I SPEND A NIGHT ON FORT HOLZER KOPJE.

ALTHOUGH an attack on the laager was highly improbable, owing to the positions of the guns already established on the kopjes, yet, I must confess, I was not without fears, and spent several restless nights in consequence. Had I known then, what I learned by observation soon after, I could have spared myself such unnecessary anxiety; for all through the campaign the poor Malabochians were seldom, if ever, the aggressors, their attitude being nothing more or less than a gentle protest against what they considered an unjust encroachment on their ancestral rights.

Had they been as strong as their neighbour Magato, our position (owing to the prevailing discontent and the fact of there being no organisation amongst the troops) would have been most critical. As it was they realised that they were the weaker and would have to give way sooner or later; hence their lack of courage. I firmly believe that had Malaboch's life been guaranteed him from the first, both he and his people would have surrendered without having fired a shot.

The Rustenburg and Zeerust commandoes had not yet joined the forces.

With reference to the want of provisions, an attempt was made to buy some Boer meal from a passing wagon, but business was prevented by the owner demanding sixty-five shillings a bag (200 lbs.). A small quantity of sugar, however, was bought at a very high figure.

The next day Laager-Commandant Schutte gave orders for the removal of the camp to a position immediately at the foot of the mountain, where a much better and purer water supply was obtainable.

A most unfortunate incident happened to-day: a number of Kafir women went to the fort (at night), which was built on the second kopje, believing it to be held by their own people. The occupants of the fort being under the impression that the enemy was attacking, fired, killing one child and taking nine women prisoners.

The report was that all food had been removed from Malaboch's kraal, and the natives were fleeing towards Zoutpansberg to seek refuge in Magato's mountain.

Arrangements were now made for the storming of Malaboch's mountain from all sides.

The Middelburgers arrived and formed a laager. All the men of the various contingents were in excellent health.

In the evening I received cheering letters from the Rev. Canon Fisher, Rev. R. J. P. Dunbar, and

LIEUT. HOLZER,
Pretoria Foot.

[*To face page* 65.

Mrs. Bousfield; they also sent a number of papers and magazines, which were very welcome.

The next morning the mountain was enveloped in smoke, so that nothing could be seen of the enemy's tactics. At an early hour, the Colonel, in charge of sixty men, started for the purpose of making another attack. After the sun had risen the smoke gradually disappeared, and the various shades of green on the mountain were very artistic. I saw many huts still burning in various places, and they formed a vivid and gruesome contrast to the otherwise peaceful appearance of Blaauwberg. Presently, through my field-glasses, I espied our artillery at the summit of one of the kopjes preparing to shell the bush.

Corporal Gert Botha received orders to proceed with twenty-one men to a kopje on the mountain, already occupied by Lieutenant Holzer and a few men; Jacques, Mauritz, and Austin were amongst those selected. Doctor Liknaitzsky and I accompanied them. We started at 11.15 A.M. on foot, taking with us each an overcoat, a blanket, and some provisions. On our arrival at noon, we found Holzer's party had already commenced to build a fort; everyone assisted in this operation, and while removing a stone, Holzer called me to look at a large scorpion, the first and only one I have ever seen. When the fort was finished, it was named, in honour of the Lieutenant, "Fort Holzer." Guards were put on all round the fort; ten of the men had gone to some deserted kraals below, and had set fire to about

F

thirty huts, the glare of which illuminated the whole kopje. They returned with many curios, such as clay-pots, calabashes, caskets, sticks of tobacco leaf, and neck ornaments. Coetzee, one of the party, brought back a necklace, quite a work of art, made from the bones of a mamba.

We had to wait a long time for water, which was some distance off. Everything was perfectly calm, not one of the enemy being visible. We made our supper off coffee and army rations, and last, but not least, the cake which Mrs. Burnham had so thoughtfully packed amongst the other nice things; very few knew of this, so that it came as a surprise, and was much appreciated. Darkness had now set in, and everybody prepared to retire, excepting of course the guards. We observed the enemy's camp-fires on a neighbouring kopje, but they were suddenly extinguished by a shell, sent in that direction by the artillery. All this was a strange experience to me, but I slept well, though our beds on the stony ground were naturally hard and rough. With convenient stones for pillows, and our topcoats for blanketing, we spent the night undisturbed in any way by the enemy, but the report of the big gun, fired at long intervals, prevented us from sleeping too soundly; we also heard in the night a most pitiful bleating, which we found in the morning to have emanated from a poor little kid.

The howling, too, of some wolves caused us some uneasiness; but we all came safely through the night,

STAATS ARTILLERY: SHOWING THE MAXIMS.

[*To face page* 66.

and anxiously awaited our relief. Early in the morning, Gerard, Jacques, Austin, and myself went out to explore. It was a very pretty spot, densely wooded, and there were wild oranges and peaches growing in the bush; ferns, too, grew in great profusion.

On a rock close by, we saw the marks of the enemy's bullets, which were fired at the skirmish already described by Austin Brook.

In a cave which we ventured into we found some tobacco leaf tied in split sticks, two of which I brought away with me. On returning to the fort we breakfasted, using as plates and spoons pieces of cardboard and chips of wood. Mauritz's plate was a piece of cracked stone.

Our relief, in charge of Sergeant Lovell Taylor, arrived at 9.30 A.M., and we at once left the kopje and reached the camp at 10.15, having been away twenty-three hours. We found everything very quiet; most of the men were busily engaged erecting tents of extraordinary shapes; they consisted of blankets of all shades of colour. News reached us that some of Mathala's men had made prisoners of several women. They killed all the children and a man, and while in the act of killing the old women they were discovered by some Boers, who immediately stopped such inhuman proceedings; they (Mathala's men) explained that it was their custom in time of war to kill all old people and boys, saving only the girls and young women. These latter were perquisites of the Chief, who, in turn, bartered them to his people as wives, taking cattle in exchange.

Adding insult to injury, they loaded their prisoners with the spoil they had taken, and drove them on before them to the camp. I saw them come in, and they were then handed over to Commandant Vorster, who took charge of them.

CHAPTER XII.

THE COMMISSARIAT.

THE next morning (Sunday), after holding service, I accompanied eight of our mess up the mountain to several deserted caves in search of curios; but there were very few to be found, some of the party brought back large baskets used by the Kafirs for carrying corn in. I found a horn full of poison and a few Kafir beads.

On the Monday, as nothing definite had been settled regarding action, most of the men went out fishing. The place selected was a most beautiful spot, the river banks being one mass of maidenhair ferns; but no fish of any consequence were caught.

On our return to camp we visited a kraal that was burned on our arrival, and found our men very busy digging; they had discovered enormous baskets of corn buried in the earth; twenty-two muid sacks full of corn were taken out of one of these baskets. The corn was very good. It was a glorious find, as our horses were almost without food.

The baskets were quite a work of art, and must have taken a long time to make. They varied in diameter from twelve to twenty-five feet.

Malaboch arranged an armistice for twenty-four

hours, promising to interview the General in the camp the next day. Mr. Schmidt, who was attached to the medical department, went into the Hoofstad, with two Kafirs, to interview the Chief. This he did at his own peril, and not by the direction of the Commandant, who declined to guarantee his safety. Everything was very quiet, not a shot had been fired all day, hostilities having temporarily ceased; we were now anxiously awaiting the arrival of Malaboch. Gerard and Jacques went to guard Fort Holzer. It was windy, and the cloud-swathed Blaauwberg presented a beautiful spectacle in the gleam of the early sunlight. I drew the Colonel's attention to it, who remarked, "I don't remember seeing anything more beautiful."

The provisions question was still exercising the minds of everybody. Upon information received, I give the following figures, which show the total amount of rations issued to Veld-Cornet Botha's Laager during the whole time they had been out from Pretoria—twenty-five days: three-quarters of a pound of coffee, a few pannikins of Boer meal, one pound of Kafir beans, one small pannikin of sugar, and five or six oranges. It will thus be seen that the rations issued by Government, if unsupplemented by private contributions, would have been quite insufficient even to maintain existence.

The result of this state of affairs was that numbers of men in this and Veld-Cornet Roos' commando openly said that they would not go up the mountain unless food was found. The Pretoria contingent, too, threatened to "strike," and had not provisions been sent the consequences would have been serious. The commissariat stores, with the exception of meat, were practically exhausted, there only being sufficient Boer meal, mealie meal, and coffee to serve as one day's rations.

It was difficult to understand how, with a force of such dimensions, the most important department (the commissariat) had been so grossly neglected; but such had proved the case, for the total supplies loaded up in Pretoria consisted, as I have already stated, of four pockets of sugar, fifteen bags of meal, a few boxes of candles, and one bag of rice (the latter almost unfit for food), and this was supposed to be sufficient for the requirements of six hundred men. Had it not been for the fact that most of the messes had privately provided themselves with extra provisions, over and above the eight days' rations expected from them, starvation pure and simple would have had to be faced when only half the journey had been accomplished. As to blankets and clothing, the amount issued was not worth mentioning. Someone had blundered, and on whomsoever the blame rested, he should have been made to suffer. But for the good temper of the majority of the men commandeered, a very serious crisis might have arisen; for it was no child's play to have to go on short rations at so early a stage in the proceedings. As it was, whilst the Pretoria men, for the most part, contented themselves with a quiet grumble (some of them, I must confess, used rather forcible language), many of the Boers openly asserted that they would go no further unless proper food was provided for them. They did go, however, after much persuasion.

Malaboch failed to keep his appointment with the General, and the armistice having expired, orders were given for the whole force, cavalry as well as infantry, to hold themselves in readiness by 2 A.M. for a combined attack on the enemy. Before retiring I held a quiet religious service in my wagon. There were present Lieutenant Holzer, Sergeants Lovell, Taylor, Kenny Shepherd, and Trooper Mauritz Preller. All the men had taken the situation seriously to heart, and anticipated disastrous results.

I received pathetic notes from some of the combatants asking me to write to mothers, sisters, and last, but not least, sweethearts, in the event of casualties.

CHAPTER XIII.

MY FIRST EXPERIENCE UNDER FIRE.

A HEAVY engagement, in which all contingents came into action, was fought to-day (June 20). At two o'clock in the morning all the men in the Pretoria Laager were paraded, and a few having been told off to secure the safety of the camp in the event of a surprise, the rest proceeded to the base of the mountain immediately below the big spur. It is almost impossible to realise the dangerous nature of this scramble. The zigzag Kafir path wound in and out of the bush, in which it would have been possible to place thousands and thousands of natives without their being seen, whilst in case of an attack, it would have been a matter of extraordinary difficulty, if not an absolute impossibility, either to advance or retreat. Had the forces been attacked with assegais by the natives during the ascent, I doubt whether one would have been left alive to tell the tale, and it puzzled me to understand why a path was chosen for us to go up, where it was necessary that we should move in single file. As it was, Providence favoured us, and we were allowed to pass through the mountainous part of the bush without being fired upon. When we had got up about seven hundred feet, the crackling of the bushes as we forced our way through them startled some baboons, and they immediately began calling to one another. This is supposed to have given the alarm to the Kafirs; but whether it was that or the blowing of a whistle a few minutes later to order our advance, I do not know. We emerged from the bush, and were collected in a group on a small flat amongst some mealie stalks from which the corn had been gathered. Here we rested and awaited orders. This brought us to the base of the kopje, which we were to take, and we were trying to find a way of ascent. I was standing on a huge boulder, Lieutenants Eloff and Holzer being a few yards in front of me, noticing a narrow pathway on the kopje, I was calling Holzer's attention to it when suddenly a volley was poured into us from the cliffs above. Clubbed together as we were in the bright moonlight, we were plainly visible, and offered a good mark to the enemy, whilst they, being concealed in crevices of the cliffs, were only discernible by the puffs of smoke from their rifles. When the first shots came whistling about our ears most of the men hurriedly placed themselves under cover. I jumped, or rather fell, off the stone on which I was standing, and ran to a much smaller one, behind which were four men lying down flat. I followed their example, keeping my head well down. While in this position a young fellow came to me with the question, "Are you lying on my cartridges?" Without raising my head I felt for them, and drew out an old pocket-handkerchief full of cartridges, which I handed to him. All this time the missiles were flying round us with a ping and a whiz, and I fancied I received one in my leg; it was only fancy, however, for it struck a young fellow named Haupt, who was lying on my right, and who marvellously escaped unhurt, it passing clean through his coat and trousers without even touching his body.

I must here mention the conduct of Veld-Cornet Botha; for as soon as the enemy opened fire, he called to his men to withdraw, and they followed him along the hill to a considerable distance. Grasping the situation, Colonel Ferreira at once gave the order to his men to advance and storm the kopje three or four hundred yards higher up to the right. The Colonel was within an ace of being shot himself, a bullet whizzing by close to his ear. Once we reached the kopje we should be practically out of immediate danger, for it was covered with tangled foliage which screened us from view. A few men were left at the foot to guard the hill, in case the Kafirs came round, in turn, to storm it. The rest clambered up to the top. As we ascended, I saw many of Botha's men, concealed in the bushes, trying to persuade the Pretoria men from going up. They said it was too dangerous, and that they would all be cut off. They were evidently surprised to see me pass, for I heard them remark, "Kijk! daar gaan de Predikant" (Look! there goes the parson). We found that a large body of natives had ensconced themselves amongst some boulders on the mountain just opposite to us, about four hundred yards away; but a heavy fire from our men forced them to beat a hasty retreat, several of them being picked off. A party of fifteen men was then sent out under Lieutenant Schroeder, and they gradually worked round a kraal to a kopje some thousand yards away, burning many huts in their progress, and being subjected to a harassing fire from the Kafirs, who, however, retreated into the bush as we advanced. A little while after, our flag was hoisted on the kopje taken by Schroeder. Adjutant Eloff was despatched with five Kafirs and three white men to take possession of the intervening ground; their advance was steadily opposed, but when the natives fell back into the bush their fire ceased, only to reopen, however, when Eloff effected the capture of some sheep. He then succeeded in joining Schroeder, from whom five men had separated, who at one time stood a very good chance of being cut off altogether, the enemy apparently closing in on them, and sending a regular hail of bullets among them.

The arrival of Eloff's little party brought a lull for the time being; and it was thought, incorrectly as it afterwards turned out, that the enemy had beaten a retreat. Having advanced so far with success, another party under command of Lieutenant Holzer was sent out, and they were afterwards joined by five men from Schroeder. Together they went fully two miles into the enemy's country, coming into fine open ground after emerging from the bush.

They were greeted with a warm fire from the very top of the mountain, but again Providence was with us, for all escaped scot-free, though one man had a big piece of the stock of his rifle shot away by a bullet from the enemy.

They ultimately managed to reach a kopje which undoubtedly held a most commanding position, the ground all round being perfectly clear; they had not long been there when a number of cattle were seen coming down the valley, and when they came up to the kop, half-a-dozen men were sent to seize them, which was successfully effected. The enemy above did all he could to prevent this capture, by keeping up a continual fire. Holzer then sent for reinforcements, and Colonel Ferreira, having left a half-dozen men to protect the big kopje, advanced himself with the rest. The Makatese struggled hard to prevent the union of the forces, but without avail; and then, twenty men being left at the kopje to cover our retreat, the rest proceeded to drive back the captured cattle. Whilst we were moving towards our original position, we were the recipients of continuous volleys from the mountain, and when half-way, came between a cross-fire, the Kafirs having got on to the hills behind us. There was a constant pit-pat as the bullets cut up the ground at our feet. Mr. Jenkins, the "Press" war correspondent, had a very narrow shave at this time; he had a white blanket rolled up and slung over his shoulders. On leaving Holzer's kopje, he was chaffed about carrying this blanket, being told that he would be a good mark for the enemy. He laughed, but sure enough a bullet went clean through the roll, and it was only its thickness that saved his life. Thus it showed how well directed was the firing to which we were subjected the whole time. We got the cattle back to our hill, and then Holzer's people started to fall back on us. They had to fight inch by inch, and it was evident that strong reinforcements had been, and were being, sent up to Malaboch. A party, consisting of Sergeant Lloyd Gates and three men, went down to get some water from a stream close by, and were assailed from all sides; so hot was the fire that they could only advance by crawling from boulder to boulder on their hands and knees. We on the top of the kopje could hear the heavy fusilade, and were in a state of great anxiety. Whilst this was happening nine men had been told off to drive the cattle down the mountain, and they started to do so. They were not allowed to proceed far, however; for having got into a kraal they were attacked on three sides.

Matters were very critical with them, but seeing that it would be impossible to attempt to get the cattle off the mountain by that path, Mr. Sutton, who had charge of the detachment, decided to try and get back to the kopje. Once more, by the hand of Providence, all returned safely.

CHAPTER XIV.

FIRST CASUALTIES.

By this time the enemy was keeping those of us who were on the kopje busily occupied by firing volley after volley on us, evidently with the idea of keeping us from sending out reinforcements, and they could be seen covering the mountain sides in swarms. The activity of Sergeant Lloyd Gates, who was endeavouring to divert their attention from the cattle party by quick firing, must, however, have puzzled them immensely, and apparently they believed that he had a strong contingent with him. Be this as it may, the cattle were brought back in safety. Realising the position of Gates, Sergeant Lever, with twenty-nine men, was sent to render him assistance; we were thankful enough when we saw them all return scatheless.

Only those who were present and saw everything could comprehend what a case of touch and go it was the whole time.

And now our position on the kopje had become so critical that a despatch was sent to Veld-Cornet Botha for reinforcements. He had spent the day building a fort in the Kafir gardens, in a position which could hardly be regarded as serviceable. He declined to send the required assistance, and, acting in his capacity as Commandant, in the absence of Commandant Erasmus, he ordered Colonel Ferreira to abandon the kopje, and retire with his men, an order which, though easy to give, was not so easily effected. We were, in fact, placed in a very critical position, and had the desired reinforcements been sent, we could have forced the enemy to retreat, and not only held our own kopje, but could have held Holzer's Kop, which gave us the command of the country for several miles on either side, and from which the chief stad could have been stormed with a certain amount of impunity ; as it was, without reinforcements, the kopje was untenable. In the meantime, the Colonel had given orders to build a fort, and every man was actively engaged in gathering stones for this purpose. While this was going on, I was, by direction of the Colonel, looking out for the enemy through my field-glasses. To get a better view, I stood on a rock, but had not been there long when bang ! bang ! and a bullet whizzed past my left ear. Down went the stones, and every man flew to his rifle. Being (of course) unarmed, I sought shelter amongst the crags of the rocks, followed by Sergeant Kenny Shepherd, who had mislaid his rifle whilst building the fort. While in this place of concealment, Kenny pointed out to me the mark on the rock where the bullet that passed me had struck. It is difficult to me to describe my feelings at this time. The most natural thing that occurred to me to do was to duck my head, which of course is very absurd. This I did, however, no less than four times that day, for I had four providential escapes before we returned to camp. In ducking, when the enemy first opened fire on us, my hat fell off; I at once scrambled for it, thinking it might be a protection for my head. Orders were then given for everybody to man the fort, a heavy firing going on from both sides the whole time. I scarcely liked the idea of leaving my place of safety, but did so. Bullet after bullet struck the stones of the fort on which the Colonel was seated. He displayed remarkable coolness and courage, and I have the greatest admiration for him. The true character of the man, as a soldier, was here exemplified, for there he sat immovable, calmly giving his orders to his men. At his invitation, I sat below him, and remained there till the firing ceased. To stay on the kopje for the night would have meant massacre; surrounded as we were on all sides by dense bush, we could not have seen the approach of the enemy until they were right on us. To come down the hill, particularly driving on the cattle in front of us, down a slope which was almost precipitous in parts, meant that, directly we reached the open, we would be exposed to a raking fire, which, under ordinary circumstances, would have accounted for most of us. We knew full well that Malaboch's men were arriving in numbers every minute, for where only one had been seen in the morning, twenty were now observable. Besides, our ammunition was running short, for we had been fighting for ten solid hours. However, there was no time to be lost, and we slowly descended, the last men on the kopje firing a few volleys to cover our retreat. There was a complete silence on the part of the Kafirs whilst we were climbing down under cover of the bush, and it was apparent that all this time they were moving parallel with us on the other side. Directly we came into the open, they, as anticipated, commenced firing. Whilst some of the men drove the cattle ahead, the others remained to return volley for volley, and I should say the Kafirs must have suffered severe loss, for after a few minutes of warm work they ceased to molest us. I am glad to say Botha's men rendered us invaluable assistance by covering our retreat, and two beautifully placed shells from the artillery must have caused the enemy further consternation. Altogether, the Pretoria contingent brought down one hundred and two head of cattle, several having been shot during the fight.

Perhaps I ought to state that Colonel Ferreira duly authorised the detachments sent out early in the day to advance only five hundred yards, but circumstances forced them to go further. The capture of the cattle was a most fortunate incident. It was five o'clock before the fighting really ceased. A man named Lombard was missing from the Pretoria laager, and we supposed him to be killed, but our suspicions were groundless, for he walked into camp later on.

Meanwhile, while matters were proceeding, as described, at our end of the mountain, the Waterberg commando had attacked the kopje on the right of the mission station, and with them were two guns. They reached the top of the hill without loss, and then advanced in the direction of the hoofstad. They were allowed to proceed some distance with nothing more than a desultory fire to face; then they were suddenly attacked on every side, and awoke to the fact that they had been entirely surrounded. The natives came on with great assurance, and the utmost difficulty was experienced in repelling them, although our fire must have created considerable panic amongst them. The Kafirs steadily closed in, and almost before the Boers realised what had occurred, the enemy had gained possession of one of the cannons, and was dragging it off. It was an exciting moment, for the Kafirs were attacking with assegais at close quarters, and a disaster seemed imminent, but pluck and nerve saved the day. Two Kafirs, who had seated themselves astride the cannon, were shot dead by one bullet, and several others fell victims to a well-timed rush. The Waterberg men recovered possession of the cannon, but from the overwhelming number of the enemy, it was seen that there was no alternative but to beat a retreat, especially as already several of our men had been wounded. So a retrograde movement commenced, and, to use the graphic language of one who was in the fight, "the path taken along the retreat was marked with blood"; for every Kafir that must have fallen, others seemed ready to take his place. The Waterberg commando fought gallantly, but it was a fight for life. If it had not been that the Kafirs were busy in our direction, it is possible that they would all have perished, and similarly, but for the Waterbergers, it is difficult to conceive what would have happened to us, for it was only after they had driven back the Waterberg people that Malaboch's reinforcements came up against us. Half-an-hour earlier the consequences would have been frightful. The Waterberg losses were: one white man killed, six seriously wounded, and ten Kafirs wounded. Amongst the wounded were two of Veld-Cornet Botha's sons; one was shot in the back, and the other in the arm.

CHAPTER XV.

THE FIRST FUNERAL.

IN the small hours of the next morning an urgent request was received in the Pretoria laager for assistance to be sent to the Waterberg Fort, as they were in great danger, and thirty mounted men were sent at daybreak. Heavy firing had been heard from that direction, and it was thought that another engagement was in progress; the kopje taken by them was the same as that where Messrs. Jenkins and Ebbage were fired on the previous day. They then noticed, as already reported, that the enemy was in force upon it, although up to then it was surmised that the Kafirs had fled to the heights. Since the reverse of the previous day the enemy had, it was stated, taken possession of all the kopjes along the face of the mountain, which were previously held by us.

Dr. Mader and Mr. Fred Neel had an exciting experience. I had called them at 2 A.M., according to a previous arrangement, and as they were not ready when the column advanced I went without them. They followed, however, later on, but somehow or other missed the road, and consequently went up the mountain about two miles to the left of us. To quote Neel's own words: "We left the laager at nine o'clock with the intention of joining your party, and when half-way up the berg came suddenly upon a large kraal, at which there were a lot of natives, two of whom were skinning a goat. These two Kafirs at once espied us, and immediately gave the alarm to their companions, whereupon numbers of them came out armed. We saw at once that retreat was out of the question, so, taking the bull by the horns, we poured in shot after shot in rapid succession, to make the natives believe we were in force. They replied with several scattered shots, and must have aimed well, as one of their bullets went clean through my hat (Neel showed me the hat with the bullet mark in it), which I had placed upon a rock beside me. They then fled, but we killed seven of them and captured nine goats, and there the goats are," and here Mr. Neel pointed to the goats, which were secured to the wagon.

The names of the wounded were as follows: R. P. Botha, in the arm; H. G. Botha, hip bone; Nel, ankle; Pistorius, foot; B. Kruger, abdomen; H. Helburg, arm.

It was reported that Malaboch had been joined by two thousand men from the chieftainess Majajie, and there appeared to be some truth in this statement, judging by the number of Kafirs engaged. It was noticed that numbers of them were armed with Martinis.

The Rustenberg commando, consisting of four hundred and sixty men, arrived to-day.

The storming of the kopje by the Pretoria contingent was undertaken on the strength of information supplied by Mr. Barend Vorster, to the effect that it was all open country at the top. This proved to be a mistake and at total variance with the truth.

After the attack on the mountain, and the excitement consequent thereon had subsided, the camp was quiet; and to relieve the monotony of our life Fred Neel suggested the publication of a cyclostyled newspaper, to contain accounts of any incidents deemed of interest to the campaigners. The first (and unfortunately the last) issue of this paper, called *The Malaboch Extinguisher*, came out on the 23rd June. Mr. Neel was an artist of no mean talent with pen and pencil, and the non-issue of this little *brochure* after its first number was keenly felt.

During this temporary lull in active operations I was cheered by receiving encouraging letters from the Bishop, Mrs. Bousfield, Canon Fisher, Rev. R. J. P. Dunbar, Mr. Burnham, Mrs. Sinclair, and others. Indeed, I looked forward with much pleasure to the mail days, and I have to tender my sincere gratitude to Mrs. Bousfield for sending me regularly the illustrated and other papers, which were much enjoyed by all.

I often accompanied the doctors on their rounds, and assisted in dressing the wounds of those maimed in the attacks on the mountain. The wounds of the brothers Botha were serious, especially that of the elder one, who was wounded in the arm. The one wounded in the hip was not in such imminent danger, the bullet having passed through his side without scarcely touching the bone. The doctor was not sure of being able to save the limb of the former.

Before retiring at night I received a telegram addressed "Rae Pretoria Laager," it ran thus:—" If does not return my oxen, run him in for theft." This puzzled me for a little time, and as no name was given I could not understand who was referred to, and when first reading it, it struck me that I had been charged with stealing the captured oxen, especially as there was a rumour in camp that many were missing. I showed it to my comrades, who advised me to return it to the postmaster in Pretoria. This I did and I heard no more of it.

The Rev. Mr. Coetsee, of Pietersburg, arrived in camp and held a service for the Dutch, returning home a few days afterwards. I held regular services every Sunday morning and evening, generally under the spacious tent of the medical officer. Nel was reported to be in a very critical condition, and while service was in progress one Sunday evening, both doctors were called away to him. After deliberating some time, they decided to amputate the injured limb. From the first the doctor held out no hope of saving it, and indeed warned the friends of Nel against delaying the amputation, saying such delay would in all probability prove fatal. His fears proved to be only too true, for the next day Nel succumbed, mortification having set in before the

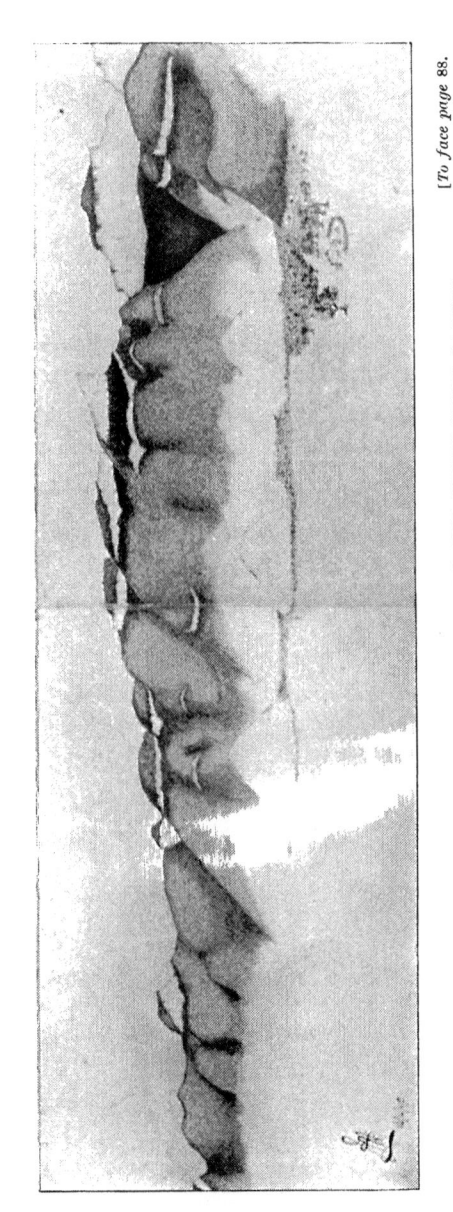

GENERAL VIEW OF BLAAUWBERG FROM THE PIETERSBURG LAAGER.

(From a Pen-and-Ink Sketch by Mr. J. Hazlehurst.)

[*To face page* 88.

operation was performed. This procrastination on the part of the Boers cost many a poor fellow his life, and was a source of trial and anxiety to the medical officer, whose advice was scarcely ever taken, no matter how bad the wound; they always waited in order to save the limb, though contrary to urgent medical advice. The doctor was helpless in the matter, and of course could not operate without first of all obtaining the consent of the friends of the patient. This was the cause of so many unsuccessful operations. There could be no doubt whatever of the skill of the warm-hearted doctor, and had he been allowed *carte blanche* the majority of his patients would have recovered. As it was, he was abused. Knowing as I did all the circumstances, I recognised the injustice done to him, who was undoubtedly, as I have already stated, most skilful in his profession. Poor Nel left a widow and seven children to mourn their loss.

Lieutenant Holzer received orders to proceed with fifty men of the infantry to the kopje which had been stormed a few days ago. They were to take provisions for two days. The party was organised and the men paraded, but just before starting, some of them had to fall out, owing to the bad condition of their boots, for they were actually walking on their bare feet. The cavalry were ordered to follow later on, the Colonel joining them just before dark. The camp was almost empty, only Charles Dargan and Mauritz Preller being left of my mess to keep me company. The night before, a grave had been dug under a maroulla tree in the camp for the reception of the remains of Nel. This was left perfectly open, without any protection whatever, and while Mr. Schmidt was on his way to visit a patient, the evening being quite dark, he fell into it, damaging his knee-cap so badly that he was unable to walk for some weeks. It caused him great pain, and he was afterwards taken to the mission station, about six miles away, where the Rev. C. Sonntag took him under his care.

The funeral service over poor Nel's body was conducted by the Revs. Coetzee and Hofmeyer, of the Dutch Reformed Church, the deceased having belonged to that denomination.

In response to a request from Malaboch, the General granted another armistice of forty-eight hours, at the same time informing him that he must surrender at the expiration of that period; but again Malaboch failed to put in an appearance. A meeting of the Krijsraad was then held, and the plan of the final advance on Malaboch's stronghold was formulated. During the sitting of this raad a petty Chief was tried for having twenty of Malaboch's oxen in his possession, while proffering friendship to us; he excused himself on the grounds that his Kafirs had found the cattle and had divided them amongst themselves, he being in ignorance as to their real ownership. He was ordered to proceed to Pietersburg by a given date, when he would be dealt with, and allotted a location at the end of the war, to which he would have to remove. The prisoner

REV. C. SONNTAG'S RESIDENCE.
Below the Mountain.

[*To face page* 90.

BURIAL OF BURGHER NEL—THE FIRST FUNERAL.

was defended by Mr. Piet Potgeiter, Commissioner of the Waterberg district, having for opposing counsel Dr. Tobias on behalf of the State.

Gauba, one of Malaboch's captains who had paid his taxes, moved down from the mountain to a temporary location.

Maniet, another captain, had also complied with the official demand.

According to reliable information the number of natives in the Hoofdstad was between five and six hundred.

In order to know whether Schmidt had really gone up to interview Maleboch, Messrs. A. C. M. Jenkins, correspondent for the "Press," and W. R. Ebbage, correspondent for "South Africa," rode to Mr. Sonntag's mission station, which lay immediately below the kopje on which was Fort Erasmus. When midway on their journey, and within about three hundred yards of the base of the mountain, they noticed numbers of Kafirs in various parts of the adjoining kopje, and were twice fired upon. On arriving at the mission station, Mr. Sonntag was found to be absent, having left at sunrise with the object of seeing Maleboch, and making a final endeavour to persuade him to come down. Whilst awaiting his return, Schmidt, who had now recovered from his accident, rode up. It appeared that, although strongly dissuaded by the missionary, he had on the previous afternoon gone up the mountain, accompanied by one of the natives, who had been sent down by the recalcitrant Chief with a flag of truce.

When he had got to within a hundred yards or so of the Hoofdstad, he sent the boy on to the kraal, to state that he wished to interview Malaboch, and asked permission to enter the stad. Malaboch returned an answer, that not having his men sufficiently in hand for him to guarantee the safety of a visitor, it would be better for him to postpone the interview until the following day, when, his followers being notified of his intended visit, would let him pass without molestation. Malaboch, however, wanted to know how it was, that whilst an armistice was proceeding the Boers had fired upon some of his men, whilst he had instructed his Kafirs that they were not to shoot as long as it lasted.

I may here say that the shooting referred to by Malaboch was indulged in by some young Boers, who, being on outpost duty, were not aware of the cessation of hostilities, and who, seeing a fire on the mountain side a short distance from their encampment, discharged their rifles in that direction.

Schmidt, disregarding advice, and against the direct orders of the Commandant, announced his intention of going to Malaboch, and left shortly after the departure of the pressmen.

He stated that from the views he had obtained from the stad, the natural facilities for its defence could not be overestimated, as in addition to being situated in a precipitous kloof, the sides of which were covered with immense boulders and thick bush, the only means of approach had been rendered practically impassable by the means of well-constructed and concealed schanzes.

Mr. Sonntag stated that Malaboch had not been down from the mountain for about three years, and was now fully determined not to yield, being of opinion that he could not rely upon the assurance of safety held out to him; Mr. Sonntag felt that all his efforts to induce the Chief to submit quietly were futile, and that a fierce resistance might be expected before the stronghold was captured.

Whilst returning to camp, Messrs. Jenkins and Ebbage were again fired at twice from the same kopje as before, but having taken the precaution to keep a respectable distance from the mountain, the bullets fell short. The result of Malaboch's failure to surrender within the specified time, was that orders were issued for a general advance at daybreak. The mountain would be scaled by the different commandoes at various points, and a keen encounter was anticipated.

A Kafir woman, who had been found by some of our men early in the day amongst the bushes, was brought into camp in the evening for medical attendance. She was in the last stage of starvation, having (as she stated) been left by her people, when they fled to the mountain, and she had had nothing to eat or drink for six days.

It was said that Malaboch's people were in fearful distress, there being no corn in the stad to feed them with, owing to their inability to reap.

One of Malaboch's men came into camp last

evening in a starving condition. He said he had eaten no food for some days. He was given a good square meal, and the next day was made use of as a guide.

Dr. Tobias and Kling left the camp with some "boys" to join the forces, taking with them provisions for the Pretorians on the mountain.

Some of our Kafirs came down from the mountain to-day (26th June), and stated that Jonker, a Pretorian, was wounded. He had entered a kraal for the purpose of loot, and, whilst thus occupied, was fired at by a Kafir sharpshooter from the top of Inswanza Krantz, the bullet entering the upper part of his right leg. Jonker fell on the open veld and lay there until pluckily brought in by Trooper Courady, who carried him on his back, under a heavy fire. Dr. Mader and Mr. Neel quickly attended to Jonker, and the next morning had him conveyed to the laager, where he speedily recovered, in spite of the non-discovery of the bullet. Soon after his return to Pretoria he suffered considerable pain. The bullet was subsequently extracted by Dr. Lingbeek, of Pretoria. Jonker, who was but eighteen years of age, is now quite well.

CHAPTER XVI.

THE COLONEL'S DREAM.

MR. FRED NEEL, who had been on the mountain for some days, returned into camp this morning; he left Dr. Mader still at the scene of operations. Neel immediately set to work to visit the patients and dress their wounds. I accompanied him, and rendered what assistance I could. We called at the tent of Veld-Cornet Botha, whose two sons, as I have already stated, were badly wounded. He was standing at the tent door, and as Neel attempted to enter, he stood in his way, refusing to let him see his sons or do anything for them, saying, "Why don't you come sooner and oftener?" He was very angry and abusive. I felt sorry for Neel, who had been exposed on the mountain, with scarcely any rest, and that morning had walked from the Pretoria Fort into the laager, a distance of about eight miles, and then, before having any refreshment himself, had attended to the wants of the wounded. To be treated with such gross ingratitude, after his self-denying labour, was indeed trying; and what is harder to bear than ingratitude!

We afterwards walked in the darkness and rain to report this to the General, who advised Neel to take no further notice of the incident. When we returned we were soaking wet to the skin, and I dined with Neel, who had not broken his fast since 9.30 A.M. (ten hours).

The weather had been wet and cold, and this tried our men very much. Austin Brook was invalided into the laager, suffering from fever caused by exposure.

It was reported that another engagement was hourly expected, but no attack had yet been made. Messrs. Vlotman, Lever, York, Claridge, and Dr. Tobias came into the camp to-day; they complained of the bitterly cold weather, and were looking very miserable; all the others they reported were well, but having a hard time of it.

The night before the Colonel left the camp he dreamed a dream as follows: "I dreamt that I had captured a red and white cow, and a black heifer; the latter had a white tip to its tail." Strange to say, this dream was fulfilled almost to the letter, for that day a cow and a heifer were captured, agreeing with this description, except that the heifer had not a white-tipped tail. Neel now had to return to the mountain to assist the doctor there. Another doctor was certainly required; for although Dr. Liknaitzky had, through the generosity of Messrs. Lewis and Marks, of Pretoria, accompanied the Pretoria contingent, and was most energetic in his attendance on the wounded, yet he could not be in two places at once. He had gone to stay for a few days in the Rustenburg Laager, a distance of about six miles from that of the Pretorians, so that at this time there was not a single medical man left in the Pretoria laager to care for the sick and wounded. Mr. Idenburg, a chemist, did much to relieve their sufferings, both by his skill and sympathy.

"*Boys*" were constantly coming down the mountain for provisions, and Mr. Elliot, the camp baker, was busy day and night baking bread and biscuits.

Messrs. Claridge, York, and Lever returned to the mountain the next day (June 29th), and on their arrival they found the Pretorians building a fort. They had just captured a kopje overlooking the head kraal. The artillery had been shelling the mountain all the morning, and the Marico men had also been firing on the kraal; the Zoutpansbergers had been busily occupied in clearing a heavily bushed kopje of the enemy.

Some hundreds of cattle were captured; it was impossible to estimate the loss of the enemy, or the effects of the bombardment, as the huts were lying amongst the boulders, and the enemy had practically deserted their town, and had fled to the rocks and caves above it. Commandant Pretorius moved, and expected a heavy day with the Pretorians on the morrow. Hand-bombs were sent to Commandant Trichardt, who intended to attack from above. The enemy was now at bay, and likely to make a desperate resistance. The Middelburgers were also within sight of the kraal, and the Marico men were trying to cut off the water. Heavy firing was going on, the enemy defending the last terrace commanding the kraal, which was to be stormed next day.

H

CHAPTER XVII.

THE CAPTURE OF CATTLE.

THE combined forces had now completely closed in around the Hoofstad, and it was only a matter of hours before it would be consigned to the flames.

Commandant Vorster and Mapen's and Kiviet's people effected a junction with the Pretoria contingent, and made a further advance, Vorster acting on the right flank, Ferreira in the centre, whilst Commandant Erasmus proceeded with a large number of Boers along a krantz to the left.

The country after leaving Fort Jonker was very beautiful, for after crossing over a nek, the road ran through a wood, which teemed with luxuriant ferns and foliage. On emerging from this we came to a fine open plain, with here and there large clumps of bush. To the rear of us, about a thousand yards away, the mountain rose clear and barren. To our left, in which direction Malaboch's stronghold lay, the hills were covered with trees and bush so thickly that the movements of the enemy there could not be observed. An advance through country of this description might naturally be supposed to be fraught with considerable danger, but strangely enough, the Pretorians never found occasion to fire a single shot, not a Kafir being seen. Some of Vorster's men, however, fired several volleys for the purpose of clearing the bush; and on reaching a suitable kopje, the nine-pounder was placed in position by Commandant Pretorius, and a number of shells were fired along the further ridge of hills, so as to displace any body of the enemy who might possibly be concealed there to oppose the progress of Erasmus and Ferreira.

At this time Vorster had reached the top of a kopje, about half a mile distant, which was supposed to cover the stad. On the other side of the hill on which was the gun, Colonel Ferreira's force succeeded in capturing about two hundred and forty head of cattle. Soon after midday, Commandant Erasmus was in full possession of the hill overlooking the stad, and was there, shortly afterwards, joined by Ferreira. During the advance along the top of the hill, Van der Venter, a Pretorian, was shot in the arm, but only a slight wound was inflicted. As no doctors were in camp, we washed the wound and dressed it with carbolic oil, and bandaged it up. Jonker had been in great pain all day, and I assisted Idenburg in giving him a morphine injection.

The stad was situated about two hundred feet from the top of the mountain, on which was the Pretoria contingent and a number of the Marico commando. It consisted of about fifty huts nestling among huge boulders, and appeared to be inaccessible save from one direction. It was evident, however, that there must be easy communication with an enormous cave, for on our arrival, although the stad was completely deserted, yet every now and again Kafirs would come out from a cleft in the rocks, and, after firing a few shots, mysteriously disappear again.

It was reported that a white man, or rather a half-cast, was fighting for Malaboch; he was said to be married to two of the Chief's women, and his brother belonged to the Middelburg laager. It was supposed that he was the marksman whose accuracy of aim at long distances had so astonished our people.

Whilst the Pretorians were making good their tenure of the hill, some desultory firing was going on just below, and in the course of this, a Middelburger named John Botha was shot through the head, death being instantaneous. He was fired at from a cave, within twenty-five yards from the spot where he was standing.

During the afternoon a continuous fire was kept up on the stad by our people, but the only result appeared to be the slaughter of four oxen, which were taken away during the night by the enemy. The Rustenburg men, who were on a kopje about half a mile away, had meanwhile trained their guns on the (supposed) mouth of the cave, and later on Commandant Pretorius, from a position on our left, did likewise, and there was a constant bombardment. This did not, however, deter the enemy from firing a few shots at a party of Kafirs, sent out from the Rustenburg fort to drive in some cattle which were grazing hard by; fortunately, no damage was done.

I ought to have mentioned that two days ago, whilst helping to drag the cannon up the kopje, one of the Rustenburg men was shot dead. I have remarked upon the almost total lack of opposition met with in our advance, and considering the firm stand made by the enemy the previous week, could only account for their altered tactics by the fact that the majority of the enemy had fled, or they had sought shelter in caves. It was quite possible that some two or three hundred of them were in the caves close to the stad, and if this were the case it showed the shortsightedness of not providing our forces with a searchlight; for then it would have been impossible for the enemy to have come out during the night, to obtain either food or water, unobserved; and their submission would have been merely a matter of days; as it was we had no check on their night foraging parties. The general opinion was, however, that Malaboch's people had scattered themselves all over the mountain, with the idea of harassing any parties of our men that might be sent down to the laager for food or ammunition. This impression was strengthened by the fact that not a single detachment had been allowed to go down the mountain without being fired upon from various points.

While Vorster's Kafirs the day before were busy trying to capture some cattle at the back of the mountain, it was observed that they were being subjected to a very warm fire, evidently directed from some caves. They were successful, however, in their efforts.

In the afternoon, whilst an ammunition party, consisting of two white men and two Kafirs (the later unarmed), were proceeding up the mountain, a shot was fired at them from a comparatively short distance. The Kafirs immediately dropped their loads and ran. A search was afterwards made for the ammunition, but without avail, and it was believed that it must have fallen into the enemy's hands. If so, they were enriched to the extent of one thousand rounds of ammunition and several hand-bombs.

This incident was the origin of a slight scare in the evening. It appeared that Commandant Pretorius sent up a red rocket, as a signal that a body of Kafirs was moving towards the base of the hill, below the forts; on this, one of the Boer Veld-Cornets threw a bombshell, which struck on a rock quite close to Ferreira's men; a few seconds after the explosion it was imagined that the enemy was beginning to use their new weapons. There was a general expression of relief when the truth became known, although, even then, it was not pleasant to think that one stood the risk of being blown to pieces by one's own people at any time.

It was reported that General Joubert was going to the fort himself in a few days, and that some further steps would be taken to stir up Malaboch.

The cliff on which the fort was situated was 2700 feet above the laager. Judging from appearances, we were much afraid that the natives were going to give us a lot of trouble, and that it would be several weeks, and possibly months, before we could say that we had thoroughly cleared them out of the mountain. Over eight hundred head of cattle were brought down from the mountain about this time; and, altogether, between one thousand five hundred and two thousand had been captured the day before.

CHAPTER XVIII.

THE REVEREND C. SONNTAG.

THERE were now several wounded men lying in the various laagers, but no hospital accommodation had yet been arranged. Jonker and Van der Venter were both of them in their respective wagons, and their comrades did all they could to relieve them of their sufferings. I used generally to visit them, when the doctor went his rounds, so as to render what assistance I could. Mr. Fred Neel was most energetic in his attentions to the wounded, and I often accompanied him to the various laagers, which were long distances apart.

On 1st July we rode to the Middelburg laager, and after dressing the wounds of the patients, we paid the Rev. C. Sonntag a visit. Mrs. Sonntag, with her children, had left the district, to escape the perils of war. Mr. Sonntag was most kind and hospitable; he informed me how much hurt he was, owing to a report in the Johannesburg and Pretoria papers, of his having given notice to the enemy of our approach by ringing the church bell. "The reports," he said, "were fabulous and altogether false. The bell, indeed, is rung every morning soon after sunrise, and has been for years; but it is only used for the purpose for which it is intended, namely, to call the people together for worship. I have done all I can to bring Maloboch to reason, even at some risk to my life. I have interviewed him three times during the last week; and, indeed, while your forces were going up, I preceded them in order to persuade the Chief to surrender; I have always upheld the Government.

Christianity, culture, and civilisation can only be promulgated under a white Government, and no matter what may have caused the war, it matters not to me; it is not for me to judge, and so I say nothing. I work for the Lord to christianise these people, and to try and make them peaceable and loyal subjects; this is my sole work, the rest I leave entirely. I have no desire to interfere in the internal affairs of the country; politics do not concern me, my work lies in another channel altogether. It is wicked, sir, very wicked, that such an infamous charge should be laid against me.

I felt for Mr. Sonntag, knowing, as I do, the trials of a missionary's life; in my opinion, there is no calling or profession that entails more self-denial, patience, and endurance than that of the native missionary. I do not altogether agree with their *modus operandi*, for I am in entire sympathy with the policy of the Government with regard to the native tribes. In bringing the natives out from their strongholds, and thus dispossessing the petty chiefs of their powers, the Government is doing a much better work than any Christian missionary has yet accomplished. While in his kraal the native lives an idle, useless life; he struts and squats about like a little demi-god, smoking insangu and drinking utyala, and otherwise satisfying his animal passions; his wives do all the work, and wait upon their lord and master, and are looked upon by him as his slaves. This is the state of affairs when the Kafir is left to himself, and the missionary works among such people. His (the missionary's) first object should be (and, indeed, must be, if any good results are to follow) to teach them that great lesson which was practised and taught by the Great Master Himself, and of which the greatest of His apostles commanded, " That if any would not work, neither should he eat." Yes, before any good can be done with these people they must be taught to work, and not to expect others to work for them. The Government is to be commended for its tact and forethought; and owing to its oneness of purpose, namely, the safety and good of the country at all hazards, it will eventually succeed. The Kafir when driven from his kraal is not left to starve, but may always find employment in the various mines at a more than fair wage; indeed, his position in this respect is even better than that of the white man, several of whom at this time, men of high standing and ability, I know to be in actual want, and who would be willing to do the most menial work to obtain a living. When the native is taught to *want*, then he will work; it is no use setting him a good example, which he will not follow; something more forcible must be done.

He must be kept under control, and subjected to discipline, and the keynote must be work! work! work!

Returning to the camp just before dark, I held service in the doctor's tent, and retired early. I could not sleep, however, as the air was filled with continuous and hideous howling; the dogs barked and the horses pranced and neighed. It was perfectly clear to us all, that there were some hungry wolves prowling about, and some even ventured inside the laager, and came quite close to the wagons: a number of the men seized their rifles, and went in pursuit. We had no sleep all night, for as soon as the chase was over, and the party had again retired, the same hideous noises were resumed, and continued until daybreak.

An amusing incident happened while we were breakfasting next morning; a tiny dog with a big head, which had been found in one of the kraals, and named Malaboch, got his head inside a small kettle, and could not get it out again. He was howling most piteously; I tried my best to extricate him, but failed. Sergeant Vlotman also tried, with the same result. At last, I held the kettle, while Vlotman pulled the dog; we were some minutes pulling and tugging, but at last succeeded in setting him free. I quite expected the animal to leave his head in the kettle, but he did not. He was soon running about again, just as though nothing had happened. "Malaboch in a kettle" became a camp by-word after that.

There was a little desultory firing going on in the mountain. I spent a very quiet day, and after retiring for the night, I heard two men quarrelling in the tent where Jonker lay. They came to a most admirable arrangement, by promising to have it out the next morning.

Most of the men in camp visited the burnt-out kraals, and commenced digging, in the hope of finding more corn for the horses, as all the other had been used, and there was no grass to speak of. After digging for some time Austin Brook succeeded in finding a haul similar to the first lot.

News was received in camp of the capture of Malaboch's father-in-law, by some of the friendly Kafirs; he was immediately sent with a flag of truce into the caves adjoining the Hoofdstad to call upon Malaboch either to surrender within twenty-four hours, or to send out all women and children, as in the event of his continuing obstinate, it was intended to blow up the caves with dynamite. The white flag was carried right up to the stad without a shot being fired by the enemy, and when the cave was reached a great number of men and women came out, and at once ran down with all available utensils to the stream near by, it being evident, from their eagerness to get water, that they were suffering terribly from the pangs of thirst. Malaboch responded to the message, that if the General would withdraw his forces from the mountain, he would come out, and asked for an extension of time in which to consider the matter, and a delay was granted of two days. Consequently, for forty-eight hours inactivity reigned; the Chief not having submitted then, hostilities recommenced. All the guns on the mountain had kept up a perpetual bombardment since sunrise, whilst in the course of the morning a Hotchkiss was brought into play by Captain Schiel.

The General was undecided whether dynamite would be made use of to finish off Malaboch, the idea being repulsive to most minds, more especially as it was thought, that, being deprived of water, he and those who were with him in the caves would be forced to submit in the course of a few days. The General gave orders that all women and children going to the water should be allowed to drink, but that all utensils for carrying water be broken; he ascended the mountain himself to inspect the various positions. Pickets were placed all along the watercourse to prevent the natives obtaining a supply, and it was, further, a matter of extreme difficulty for the Kafirs to leave the caves under the heavy fire of the cannon.

Malaboch's relative informed us, prior to taking in the flag of truce, that there were over four hundred of the tribe seeking shelter in the caves, and it was thought, if the statement were reliable, that, with either their extinction or their submission, the campaign would be brought to a speedy termination.

Adjutant Sarel Eloff, whose leave from Government had expired, left to-day (5th July) for Pretoria, accompanied by Sergeant-Major Malan. Young Eloff had made himself popular by his gentlemanly bearing to all and self-possession while under fire.

Flags of truce were again seen, and, under cover of these, Lieutenant Schroeder and six men went on to the top of the kopje above the cave, for the purpose of finding a good place in which to operate with dynamite. With regard to the lamentable lack of clothing and boots, there were still numbers of the Pretoria men practically unfit for duty, owing to their being almost barefooted, although other laagers had been practically provided with all necessaries. I was utterly at a loss to understand why partiality should be shown in this matter.

There was now a fair supply of provisions, but these came none too early.

There was a report in camp that Magato's people had attacked some whites in the Zoutpansberg district, but this proved to be camp gossip.

A supply of medical comforts, kindly sent by Mr. Sam. Marks, was received by Dr. Liknaitzky, who divided them with Dr. Mader.

All the wounded were progressing favourably.

The dynamite had arrived, and Commandant Pretorius was trying to obtain men to place it in position. Six men of the Pretoria laager were eventually engaged by the General for that purpose; and on their guaranteeing the effectiveness of their charges, they were promised one hundred pounds each.

Three different spots were selected, one immediately

above the Hoofdstad, and the others on either side of the krantz overhanging it.

While some of Mathaba's Kafirs, who were in charge of two artillerymen, were engaged in cutting a path to a spot where Maláboch's people had been in the habit of obtaining water during the night, they were fired upon by the enemy, and two of them were wounded. The remainder took to their heels, leaving behind them three rifles and two axes; these, however, were recovered shortly afterwards.

By means of a powerful telescope, which had been placed on the top of the kopje where the mountain gun was in position, an excellent view of the interior of the cave was obtainable, and it was observed that although the majority of the shells exploded were well within the entrance, but few casualties ensued, no Kafirs being visible during the cannonading; from this fact it was presumed that the cave was of considerable extent, the more so, as the number of natives seen airing themselves on the adjoining ledges, during the temporary cessation of hostilities, had been computed at not less than one thousand. About two hundred Kafirs of the Waterberg laager passed through that of the Pretorian's on their way to the General to get their leave. They went through many manœuvres, using their knives, hatchets, assegais, and rifles. They had just caught an imaginary prisoner and were hacking him to death. They looked very fiendish in their general get-up, feathers in their wool, and paint on their faces, and the war horns sounding at short intervals. Some had their faces whitened and were yelling horribly; had they fought in this manner, when in active service, they would have been most useful to us; but such was not the case, they were arrant cowards, and always fled as soon as they heard a shot fired by the enemy.

In the evening, those of the Boers who were left in the laager were singing the Old Hundredth in most doleful strains, and it struck me as being quite out of place under such circumstances. We were in constant fear of being attacked by the routed enemy, who was fleeing in all directions; and as there is a time for everything, this was the time to be on the alert, to prevent a catastrophe, and not to be lying on one's back singing. Had we been attacked, we should all have been massacred without the least doubt.

RENO.   STEER.   CLARKE.   MAYNARD.   INGLE.
THE COMMANDEERED PRISONERS AND THEIR GUARDS.
(*From a photograph by Exton.*)

[*To face page* 113.

CHAPTER XIX.

I VISIT THE PRETORIA FORT.

The commandeered prisoners already mentioned arrived with their guard this evening (6th July) none the worse for their journey; indeed, they were looking well and happy. They had no complaints to make. Young Mr. Kruger, the officer in charge, had been true to his promise of fair play; in fact, they were probably better off than those who came up willingly, as their many sympathisers had tendered most substantial aid. They occupied an empty tent near my wagon, just vacated by Eloff and Malan. In the evening a vocal and instrumental concert was held by them, one of their number being an adept banjoist.

During the engagement of the previous day some of our men were reported killed, and others wounded. I therefore decided to ascend the mountain, so as to render what assistance I could, and to hold a religious service. Messrs. Brook, Loveday, and Watkins were going up the next day, so I availed myself of their company. We started at 3.30 A.M., passing through the artillery camp *en route*. Here I noticed, to my surprise, more than a hundred Kafirs, armed with assegais and knobkerries, at this early hour,

On enquiry, I found they had been engaged to transport fifty-three boxes (each fifty pounds) of dynamite to the Pretoria fort, situated just above the Hoofdstad, the object being to blow up the caves. I must acknowledge that this procession of one hundred yards or so of dynamite, carried along by sleepy, careless Kafirs, caused me more uneasiness than had the enemy in all his exploits. At 4.30, fifty-three of the Kafirs each lifted a case of dynamite on to his head and filed off, while the remainder walked behind to act as a relief party. It was a tremendous climb, and one I shall never forget. Here, again, I may mention the want of strategy on the part of the enemy, for had one shot been correctly aimed from amongst the dense bush surrounding us, so as to touch off the dynamite, the transport party would have been simply annihilated, chaplain included.

The mountain scenery, as we ascended, was very lovely; indeed, I do not remember seeing finer vistas of bush-clad kloof and berg anywhere. Presently we passed a level, grassy plateau, intersected by streams of limpid water, and anon, we entered a wild ravine, the sides water-worn by mountain torrents. Our progress was hindered by boulders of all shapes and sizes in chaotic confusion. Owing to the enemy allowing us to proceed unmolested, I was able to drink in, as it were, the natural beauty and grandeur of our immediate surroundings. But my admiration of the scenery was rudely disturbed, and my thoughts brought back suddenly to the "realities of war" by a

STAATS ARTILLERY CAMP: BLAAUWBERG IN BACKGROUND.

[To face page 114.

Kafir clumsily dropping a box of dynamite. Most fortunately, the imminent explosion did not come off, and after warning the Kafir (and the others as well) of the disaster so nearly brought about by his carelessness, we again proceeded, watching the bearers now very strictly, as life or death to the whole party was literally in the hands of each and all of them. It was a relief when, still whole, and in one piece, we reached the fort, the journey having occupied some six hours.

I found the fort to have been extremely well chosen as regards position. It was practically impregnable from the Hoofdstad below, owing to protecting and almost overhanging boulders and pinnacles of rock : we were thus secured from the enemy's fire as long as we remained *in the fort*; but to venture, through curiosity, outside our natural fortifications, was attended with great danger. As evidence, I found that Van der Merwe, of the Middelburg laager, while trying to get a view of the Hoofdstad, had been shot through the head shortly before our arrival, death being instantaneous. I was much affected on hearing this, as poor Van der Merwe, before going up the mountain, had come to wish me good-bye. He was suffering from a very bad cold, and could only speak in a whisper. I reminded him of his weak condition, and begged him to take as much care of himself as the circumstances would allow. He treated the matter very lightly, saying he would be allright. I wished him Godspeed, and we parted for the last time.

Whilst General Joubert was standing on a rock looking down upon the Hoofdstad to decide upon the best spot on which to lay the dynamite, he was fired at by the Kafirs, and narrowly escaped being killed, the bullet passing close to his head, and striking a rock immediately behind him.

I heard that Malaboch had sent an elephant's tusk to the General as a tribute of peace, and asked for an hour and a half's time in which to surrender. This led to further parley, during which Malaboch expressed himself as willing to yield if a guarantee were given him that his life would be spared. He said he did not want to fight, but was frightened he would be killed if he gave himself up. No guarantee could be given him, and as, by the end of the time granted, he had not come out of his hiding-place, hostilities were recommenced. Whilst, however, the truce was in force, D. Kraft, of the Pretoria contingent, was wounded. He was on picket duty on a ridge just above the stad, and to the right of the Pretoria fort. Wishing to obtain a better view of the enemy's stronghold, he exposed himself, and instantly received a reminder from below in the shape of a bullet, which grazed his neck, inflicting a flesh wound.

Lieutenant Schroeder, with the six men deputed to lay the dynamite, had been mining on a spot supposed to be immediately above the caves, and which had been selected on the advice of Colonel Ferreira. Directly the interval asked for by Malaboch had expired, preparations were made for the explosion of

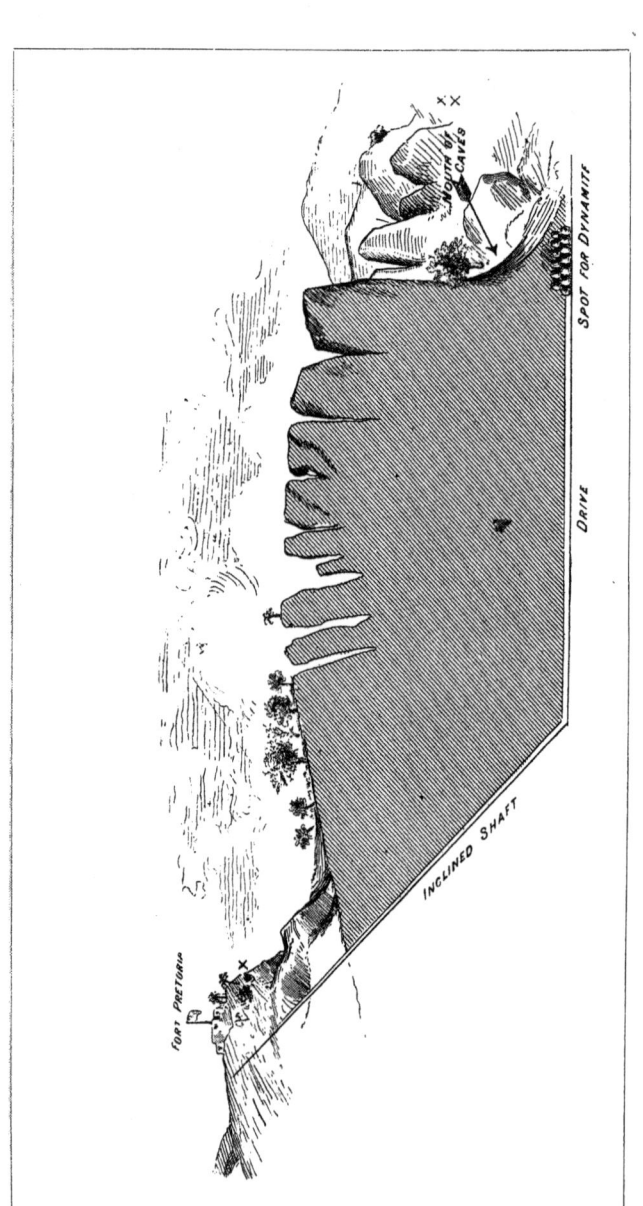

PLAN OF PROPOSED BLOWING-UP OF MALABOCH'S CAVES. (By F. NEEL.)
(* Kraft shot here. ** Le Clercq shot.)

[To face page 117.

a charge of three hundred and fifty pounds of dynamite. The fuse was laid, and then the bugle sounded the signal for everybody to leave the fort and place themselves out of harm's way. Scarcely had the first note been blown than there was a general helter-skelter, the main idea of everybody being to get as far away as possible. Lieutenant Schroeder remained behind a few minutes to fire the fuse, three and a half minutes being allowed before the explosion; but several of the Pretoria men preferred to remain in the fort, and seek safety under overhanging rocks. Colonel Ferreira, with a number of others, stood on a crag about two hundred and fifty yards away from the spot where this monster charge was laid, and prepared to await the effects of the explosion. Those three and a half minutes seemed very long, but at last a tremendous cloud of smoke and dust, accompanied by a report similar to that which might be expected if a dozen one hundred-ton guns were fired simultaneously, announced that the exciting moment had come. Far up into the air shot huge fragments of rock, so high, that at last they were almost lost to sight, and then they descended with a whistling sound that was not pleasant to hear. Although pieces fell in all directions, none of our people were hurt.

On visiting the scene of the explosion, it was discovered, that though a considerable portion of the krantz had been shifted, and a lot of huts crushed under the *débris*, the cave itself did not appear to have sustained any actual damage. A fort was then built on the spot, and was garrisoned by the Marico contingent.

Desultory firing had been going on all round, the Kafirs replying from time to time, with apparently no better results than characterised our efforts. This was due to the fact that we could not see the enemy, hidden as he always was by bush and boulders. In the course of the morning two more forts had been thrown up on a spur, on the extreme left front, some two hundred feet below Fort Pretoria and five hundred yards from the Hoofdstad. Some idea of the hazardous position in which the occupants were placed may be formed from the fact, that a youth named Van der Westhuizen was wounded in the wrist and chin soon after his arrival there. Thirty men under the command of Lieutenant Rice now held the forts. The result of the skirmish was, one man killed and five wounded; the names being: killed, Van der Merwe, Middelburg; wounded, Van der Westhuizen, Middelburg; D. Kraft, Pretoria, Lottering Artillery; Townsend, Marabastad; Coetzee, Rhenosterpoort.

The detachment with Lieutenant Rice spent a most wretched night in the fort, owing to their being continually harassed by the enemy, who was evidently endeavouring to surround our position, an intention which was defeated by several well-directed volleys. They were standing to arms the greater part of the night, and what with the constant throwing of hand-bombs from the various small forts, rocket-firing from the artillery, and the occasional bursting in their vicinity of a misdirected shell, matters were lively, and rendered sleep out of the question; another man was shot dead through the neck, close to the spot where Van der Merwe was killed. It was intended to remove the Pretoria laager from its present site, but in consequence of a message being sent down, that the war was likely to be over in a few days, nothing was done in that direction, although there was nothing to warrant hopes of such a speedy termination of the campaign; for whilst we were losing at the rate of two or three men a day, the enemy, so far as we knew, was escaping "scot-free."

Dr. Tobias escorted me to the fort occupied by Lieutenant Rice and his party; we reached the fort without being fired on, and there I saw Messrs. Dutoit, Gert Botha, and Taylor, and stayed with them for some time.

On returning to the Pretoria fort, we found that preparations were being made for firing a second dynamite charge. The arrangements for safety of the firing party, time, fuse, etc., were similar to those made for the previous explosion, except that two hundred pounds of dynamite, instead of three hundred and fifty, were fired. As this second charge did not have the desired effect, it was decided to try another charge of fifty pounds in the hope of tumbling over a large piece of the krantz. The usual signal was given for everyone to get away as far as possible; but the only result was a tremendous report, and a small piece of rock shot up into the air, and descended with great force close to where I was standing. The failure was ascribed to the fact that the rocks were composed of sandstone, which, being of a yielding nature, did not afford a sufficient amount of resistance to the explosive. On this account, it was doubtful whether any further experiments would be made with dynamite.

Our list of casualties continued to swell; three more Kafirs were wounded. One of the Middelburg contingent had a very narrow escape of being shot in the shoulder, the bullet passing through his coat. Up to this time our loss was about six whites killed, twenty-one wounded; fifteen Kafirs killed, thirty wounded. An effort had been made to burn down the bush, and this had been going on for several days. The burning had the effect of driving the enemy from his places of concealment; but it also destroyed a most charming feature of the landscape, giving a black barren appearance to what had been wooded kloof and donga—a fitting emblem of the blighting influence of war. During the day, the Rev. C. Sonntag informed the General that the previous night Malaboch had sent a messenger asking him for an interview; but although permission was given to Mr. Sonntag to take in a flag of truce, and see whether he could not prevail upon Malaboch to surrender before more harm was done, he preferred not to run the risk.

The General left the mountain a few hours after my arrival there, but before doing so he addressed the burghers, saying that after the way Malaboch had behaved, he had decided to take no further notice of any flag of truce which might be sent out by him; the only one he would recognise would be that carried by Malaboch himself. At the same time he recommended the Boers to confine their whole attention to the Kafirs, and not to fowls and dogs, as each specimen of the feathered tribe that had been shot, had cost the Government at least four pounds, while the canine corpses would represent as much as twenty pounds apiece; for the future he hoped they would desist from such a wreckless waste of ammunition.

Continuous firing was being kept up from the fort; this was not responded to by the enemy.

Feeling tired, I sought rest very early, my bed consisting of a thin blanket stretched upon the rocky ground. I lay between Mauritz Preller and Austin Brook, there being only one blanket, and an overcoat (the latter kindly lent me by Sergeant Van der Bijl) between the three of us. The two outer men were alternately warm, and shivering, as the blanket was pulled hither and thither, while the man in the centre (myself) was fairly well off all the time. Though dead beat, we had little sleep; in the middle of the night we were all disturbed by the thud of a bullet, which fell close to the smouldering embers of the fire. I shouted out, "What's that?" and Austin replied, sleepily, "A bullet, I suppose," and went fast asleep again. Lieutenant Schroeder and some others at once jumped up, the former throwing two hand-bombs, one of which he let fall after being lighted. In a second he picked it up and threw it towards the Hoofstad; no sooner had it left his hand than it exploded with a bang: fortunately no one was hurt.

Before I had retired, curiosity had prompted me to peer through a crevice in the rocks, and I was able to see right into the enemy's stronghold, which was illuminated by a large fire.

Firing recommenced at daylight, and one of the Waterburgers was shot in the abdomen whilst going down to fetch water; he expired before he could be taken into the laager.

I held divine service at nine o'clock, preaching upon the subject of death. I was thinking much of poor Van der Merwe, and, indeed, of all who had been killed in the various actions; and as I looked at the bareheaded assembly before me (about four hundred) I was much impressed with the solemnity of the occasion. All present were visibly affected, not in consequence of the dangers surrounding us, but in thinking of the bereaved widows and orphans. The most hard-hearted would have found it difficult, under the circumstances, not to have been touched on hearing the strains of those pathetic lines, "Days and moments quickly flying," "When our heads are bowed with woe," and "Brief life is here our portion," sung by this vast assembly of brave men. During the whole of the service a tremendous firing was going on from all sides, the artillery sending in shells from the Maxims in rapid succession; and I must acknowledge feeling a little distressed while preaching, expecting every moment to be knocked over, for the enemy's bullets whizzed over our heads, sometimes in too close proximity to be pleasant, and causing us to duck our heads at intervals. At the conclusion of the service I was besieged by my comrades, who thanked me for the sympathetic words I had uttered. This spirit of gratitude for the least kindness shown prevailed from the beginning to the end of the campaign, and made a rough life (for, indeed, it was rough) quite easy to be borne.

I left the mountain shortly afterwards, being escorted by Messrs. Watkins and Brook. On reaching the plateau already described, whilst we were quenching our thirst at one of the streams, we heard the report of a gun on the mountain at a distance of about three hundred and fifty yards. Later on we came to the mealie gardens, where I first experienced being under fire, and there I examined the rock on which I stood and from which I fell. The place was quiet enough now though, as all the Kafirs had fled to their Chief for safety.

CHAPTER XX.

MORE CASUALTIES—DEATH OF SCHMIDT.

CAMP-LIFE now became very monotonous, and the men talked of nothing but home, and were anxiously awaiting the relieving commandoes. Orders were again given to shift the camp, and the wagons had all been emptied and everything repacked, when the order was again countermanded.

I rode with Neel to the Middelburg laager to see the wounded, and on returning enjoyed a rubber of whist with Captain White (late B. B. P.) and Messrs. Jenkins and Stubbs.

The next morning we heard a loud report from the mountain, and soon after saw a cloud of smoke rise up; this was the result of another charge of dynamite being fired.

In the evening I rode with Corporal Vlok to the hospital to visit poor Lottering, who was very bad, mortification having set in. He was quite conscious, and expressed his gratitude for my call.

Some of our men had come down from the mountain for a few days. In order to relieve the monotony, Corporal George Waldeck, who had accidentally hurt his hand, and was therefore incapacitated from duty, asked if there were any in the camp who could run, saying that if there were, he would give any of them ten yards out of a hundred and run away from them easily. The winner was to receive ten shillings, the loser paying it. Mauritz Preller accepted the challenge, and Lieutenant Rice was the starter. The runners toed the line, and "Go" was given, and off Mauritz bounded like a deer. Waldeck turned, and ran away from him in an opposite direction. Hence, Mauritz lost his bet, but payment was not insisted on.

The commandeered prisoners now received twenty-four hours' notice to leave the camp, and they at once left for Pietersburg in a special wagon which they chartered for that purpose. I again received cheering letters from Mrs. Bousfield, the Rev. R. J. P. Dunbar, Mr. Burnham, Mrs. Sinclair, and other friends.

Whilst we were idling in the camp, our comrades on the mountain were busy enough. Lieutenant Schroeder, taking with him thirty Pretorians, under orders from Acting-Commandant Uijs, went to assist Commandant Vorster's Kafirs in throwing up a fort, with the object of cutting off the water supply previously referred to. Schroeder applied to each of the Veld-Cornets of the Pretoria District to give him ten men to strengthen the detachment, but they declined. Our men were first marched to Fort Henning, and thence they went down with forty Kafirs to the place where it was intended to build the fort. Small parties of the Zoutpansbergers were told off to occupy a ridge on the left of Fort Henning, which ran at right angles, thus covering the operations of the building party. Before the desired spot was reached, it was necessary for our men to break their way through very dense bush, but after this they came into a large open space, where they were at once exposed to any fire which might be directed at them from the krantz, which was only a couple of hundred yards away. Further on a parapet was thrown up so as to afford the men a shelter, and behind this they immediately esconced themselves. Under cover from our men and the Zoutpansberg people, the friendly Kafirs brought stones to build the wall up higher; but this had not been in progress long, the front tier of the fort being about half built up, when the Pretorians were startled by seeing their native allies rush into their midst. This was caused by one of their party being wounded in the feet, and one shot dead through the neck. Not long after, one of Malaboch's Kafirs, who had been taken prisoner the previous day by Vorster's men, fell fatally wounded through the back. A number of the now panic-stricken Kafirs decamped, leaving the Pretorians in the lurch, who, notwithstanding this, and regardless that a perfect hail of bullets was being poured in upon them, pluckily continued, themselves, to complete the fort. In the meantime, the Zoutpansberg burghers had retired from the ridge by order of Commandant Vorster, on account of the hot fire they were subjected to. After this there was a lull in the firing, and suspicion was aroused that some cunning scheme was on foot to which it was intended our men should fall victims.

At 4.15, Lieutenant Schroeder gave the order to retire as speedily as possible to Fort Henning. It was remarkable, that during all this time the guns at that fort, which were supposed to cover our people, were silent; but the startling discovery was made, on the return of the men, that there were only three shells left in the fort at the time the order was given to fall back. Six men were appointed to act as rearguard, viz., J. Schmidt, W. Keith, Hendrik Smit, J. C. Dunsdon, George Scobel, and F. P. Cowley. Not many yards had been covered when J. Schmidt fell, having been shot by a bullet, which smashed two of the bullets in his bandolier, and glanced off, making a terrible wound in his loin, from whence blood flowed freely. The cry that one of ours was down passed along the line, and a loyal response was made. Several men who had already reached the fort rushed back (unarmed) with a stretcher to bring him in. In the meantime, the rearguard were making the best of their way back to the fort, which was only about one hundred yards distant, when they found themselves in the midst of an ambuscade, the marksmen being not more than a dozen yards away from them. Dunsdon fell, struck on the one side by a bullet, and on the other by a charge of buckshot; the handle of an axe which he was carrying was smashed to splinters. Immediately after, Cowley was shot through the stomach, the ball entering one side and coming out the other. The situation of Scobel and Keith now became very critical, more especially as the former had his rifle jammed with an empty cartridge, and Keith's supply of ammunition was reduced to two rounds. Hendrik Smit distinguished himself by first returning empty-handed to assist his comrades. On grasping the situation, he went a few yards back along the path, and, snatching a rifle from the hands of another man, was just in time to shoot a Kafir, who was covering Scobel and Keith. A lot of the Pretorians, upon hearing the cries for assistance, rushed down to their aid. Lieutenant Schroeder and Carl Schmidt succeeded in rescuing Dunsdon, while Cowley, better known to the troopers as "Kafir Jack," at once rose to his feet, and returned unaided to the fort. During the retreat, the enemy, now jubilant, was closing in, making the air ring with their yells and war-horns, and charging through the undergrowth so as to surround the men, pouring in, at the same time, volley after volley, on the plucky little band struggling to reach the fort. They actually came to within forty yards of the fort, being all the time under protection of the bush, and succeeded in shooting another of our men (Loveday) whilst he was standing close to the mountain-gun. The bullet passed through his thigh, fortunately without touching the bone. The wounded were dragged in safety behind the stone barricades which had been thrown up. In response to the enemy's fire, whose bullets flattened themselves against the huge boulders in the middle of the fort, a brisk fire was opened by our people; this and a charge of grape-shot, fired by Lieutenant Wolmarans, had the effect of dislodging the enemy from the east flank, who was ultimately driven back on all sides.

The sun had not yet gone down, so, by the aid of the heliograph, medical assistance was requested. Dr. Liknaitzky lost no time in answering the appeal, and arrived about dusk, escorted by six men. He attended to the wounded, Mr. Julius Fuchs rendering valuable assistance. Poor Schmidt's condition, however, had become very precarious, and owing to the great loss of blood he succumbed, without having spoken. He was born in Baden, Germany, and was only nineteen years of age : being held in high esteem, he acted as standard-bearer on this occasion.

Lieutenant Schroeder was of opinion that to return that night to Fort Pretoria was out of the question, as it was almost certain that the paths would be blocked up by the enemy ; also, the wounded could not be deserted, and it was possible that Commandant Vorster might require aid. Pickets were, therefore, placed on all sides within the fort and the walls were strengthened. The Pretorians were not very comfortably situated, as originally they had only been ordered out for six hours, and went without rations or blankets. Commandant Vorster's men and the artillery did all they could with the scanty means at their disposal to make things pleasant. The night passed in safety, though sleep was out of the question. The next morning a search party went into the bush to try to discover the two rifles which had been lost by Schmidt and Dunsdon at the time they were shot ; but they could not be found, they had evidently fallen into the enemy's hands. During the search, the party came across the body of the unfortunate Malaboch prisoner, who had been killed, and saw with horror that his right arm had been cut off, and the corpse skinned.

I may here mention that it was only on returning from the fray that it was known into what a death-trap our men had been taken. On the previous night a picket was called out to guard a footpath in the vicinity of Fort Henning, by which a number of Kafirs were endeavouring to escape. They captured, among other prisoners, a young girl, who stated that a large number of young bloods had been told off to guard this particular position, the water obtainable there being their last hope. Two parties of our men had already been nearly cut off there. She also stated that Malaboch's natives were not at all scared by the dynamite, nor the hand-bombs; the only things which they feared, and could not understand, were the rockets. A great number of the natives, she said, had died in the stronghold of hunger and thirst, but the Chief would not give in, as he was afraid to trust himself to the Boers.

I believe it can be taken as a fact, that had the order to retire been delayed ten minutes by Lieutenant Schroeder, not one of the men engaged would have come out alive. They would have been entirely surrounded and massacred. After the search party had returned to the fort, sixteen men were told off to escort the dead and wounded to the laager, while the remainder returned to Fort Pretoria. Rough stretchers were immediately constructed, the patients placed upon them, and the journey to the laager was commenced; a number of Malitses men acted as bearers. Scarcely three hundred yards had been traversed, however, when the enemy, who had come from the Hoofdstad, crept down into the bush and fired upon them. The bearers dropped their burdens and sought shelter behind stones, but by dint of kicks and threats to shoot them, they were induced again to proceed. It was an exciting moment, for the enemy's fire had to be returned; but luckily, Captain Schiel's fort was within easy distance, and running the gauntlet of the Kafirs' fusilade, they made a dash for it (that is, for Captain Schiel's fort), and reached there in safety. When Cowley was dropped, he managed to get up and hobble along without assistance.

The Rustenburg laager was at last reached, and our men, who had been on duty (some of them) forty-eight hours, with little rest or food, were hospitably entertained, and a light wagon was procured for the wounded. The party safely reached our laager shortly after sundown.

The following are the names of those who were engaged in this action: Lieutenant Schroeder, F. Cowley, J. Strauss, junr., D. Coetzee, B. Yorke, B. Bodes, P. Rothmann, W. Keith, H. Loveday, E. Wadsworth, F. Acton, W. Ramsay, J. C. Dunsdon, K. Schmidt, Fred. McArthur, C. Goodhouse, George Scobel, W. van den Berg, J. van der Berg, J. Schmidt, E. Roehlin, Julius Fuchs, A. Horsom, P. van Vuren, M. van Vuren, S. van Vuren, S. Schmidt, S. Emmenes, J. Papenfus, H. Smit, B. Pelzer, M. Booysen, and A. van der Westhuizen.

About noonday, a number of huts in the stad were ignited, and the conflagration continued all night. Owing to a report that Fort Jonker had been attacked, a relief party was sent there; but it appeared that, during the night, a large fire had been noticed about five hundred yards away, and several shots were fired at it, with the result that it was put out. On going to the fort, the spoors of two horses, and of a large number of Kafirs, were found at the spot, so it was presumed either that reinforcements had arrived from elsewhere, or that Malaboch's Kafirs were returning to him. Some of our prisoners informed us that traders living in the vicinity of Malaboch, and on the Spelonken, had been supplying the Chief with ammunition and rifles; but this was scarcely thought possible.

CHAPTER XXI.

THE HOSPITAL.

THE Commissariat Department was still a source of grumbling. Very little desire was evinced by this department to do justice to the Pretoria contingent, for whilst clothes had been served out to all the other laagers, most of the Pretoria men were still without necessaries, and after being sent from pillar to post, they were again put off. The General himself had seen that some of the men were provided for, but the majority had, owing to some one's incapacity or indifference, to get on as best they could.

We were, by this time, pursuing a policy of inactivity, although another attempt was made to block up the entrance to the cave adjoining the Hoofdstad, by means of blowing up the overhanging ledge with dynamite. The operation, however, was not more successful than the previous ones had been. One of the dynamitards, Joe Morris, was slightly hurt by a piece of falling rock, being struck on the head, and receiving a scalp wound. An attempt was made to set the huts on fire, by sending a few explosive rockets among them, but the only effect this had was to bring a few of the Kafirs out from their hiding-place, and a few stray shots were fired at our people above, without any harm being done. Then Captain Schiel experimented with some shells filled with rags soaked in paraffin, and these proved more effective, two or three huts being ignited by them. An old Kafir woman who had been captured, stated that most of the natives had fled to a Chief close by, and that only Malaboch and a few of his indunas were left in the cave which we were bombarding; but this information was taken " cum grano salis."

The women and children were escaping nightly, but it was thought, from what had already occurred, that Malaboch would not give in without a desperate struggle. Every night there was a fight at the water, and on one of these occasions three women were unfortunately shot. They were seen gliding amongst the bushes, and were naturally mistaken for men. During the last dynamite experiment, it was discovered that there was another stream of water near the cave which the enemy had been able to use, so that, apparently, they had been but little affected by our efforts to cut off their main water supply.

The next morning, on paying my visitation to the wounded, I was agreeably surprised to find that a number of tents had been enclosed by a scherm. Dr. Mader, the chief medical officer, had now organised a proper medical staff, and everything possible was being done to alleviate the sufferings of the sick and wounded. The doctor informed me that a large order had been given for a further supply of necessaries. At this time there were only three patients in the hospital itself. They were Messrs.

Lottering, Van der Westhuizen, and Townsend, all of the artillery. Lottering had received a terrible wound, and his recovery was considered very doubtful. The bullet had entered at the elbow, and passed completely up the arm, smashing the bone to splinters, and finally passing out at the shoulder. For a long time the doctor was unable to trace the passage of the bullet, having no probe sufficiently long for the purpose. He was almost abandoning the search as futile, when his able assistant, Mr. Fred Neel, suggested using a ramrod, and at last, after almost three hours of intense anxiety, success crowned their efforts. Tubing was then attached to the top of the rod, and carefully drawn through, so that a constant current of filtered water was enabled to be kept running through the shattered limb. Amputation was impossible, so that if Lottering's life was saved his arm also would be, and it was gratifying to notice the progress he made daily.

Van der Westhuizen, who also had his arm shattered, was getting along well, and thought to be out of danger. Townsend, who was shot in the leg, was almost well. Our other wounded men were all up and doing well, Jonker and the two Bothas being almost convalescent. Mr. Idenberg, who was now attached to the medical staff, rendered valuable assistance to the doctors.

Much had been said with regard to the hospital accommodation, and the want of sufficient medical attendance; but there could now be no possible room for cavil, for whilst Dr. Mader, Mr. Neel, and staff were located at the hospital, Dr. Liknaitzky was on the mountain to render such services as might be required before the wounded were sent down to the hospital.

A somewhat exciting adventure befell Corporal Vlok, of the Pretoria contingent. In the course of the morning of July 6th, he left the laager with two others to go to the Pretoria fort. They jogged slowly along, intending to go up by the path leading past the Rustenburg position; but a dispute arose, and eventually his companions returned to camp, leaving Vlok to pursue the rest of the journey alone. From this point, I use his own words :—

"I struck into a footpath which, being well worn, appeared to me to be the path taken by our people in going up to the fort. I had not proceeded far though when I met one of the friendly Kafirs, coming down to fetch water, who told me that I must not continue on that path, as the enemy was all around. I did not take any notice of this information, and after sitting down to have a pipe, went on.

It was now about four o'clock; the path took me into a dense forest, the trees being so tall and overhanging that it was impossible to see the sky above. I had travelled a long distance through the bush, and was still quite unconcerned, when suddenly a bullet came whistling past me, and flattened itself against a rock at my side.

I could only note the direction from which the shot came, for I could *see* nothing to alarm me, but I stooped and picked up the bullet, so as to keep it as a curiosity. I had scarcely done so, when two others came over my head, and I then put a cartridge in my gun to return the fire; to my horror it missed fire, and each of the remaining four rounds left in my belt did the same. I then thought it best to retreat, and scrambled over a rock, when another bullet flew past me; but although I tried each of the five rounds three times over, I could not get them to go off, my gun having suddenly for some unaccountable reason got out of working order. I remained behind that rock for over half-an-hour, my only feeling being one of intense loneliness, for I expected every moment to be attacked by the Kafirs with their assegais; and although I had made up my mind to defend myself to the last with the rifle itself, I could not help thinking that if I fell none of my comrades would know what had become of me, and still worse, there was the dread of being wounded and left alone in the midst of the bush to die of thirst. I had to make a move one way or the other, so at last I determined to push forward, and ultimately, just as the sun was setting, I emerged from the bush; as I did so, I heard a voice far up on the cliffs above me, calling, and I recognised some Boers. They wanted me to climb up the mountain to where there was a fort; but although I thanked them very much for their offer to cover me in my attempt to scale the cliff, I felt that in my tired state it was impossible for me to carry out their advice, and disregarding their warning, I preferred to go on. Then I reached the water picket, who in turn tried to dissuade me from going further; but finding me bent on reaching the Pretoria fort, they pointed out the path, and advised me to run as quickly as possible. I did not run, but walked pretty fast, and I cannot tell you how glad I was when at nine o'clock I found myself in the midst of our fellows. So glad was I, that I wanted to shake hands with my nigger, but the poor beggar wouldn't let me."

CHAPTER XXII.

HONOUR TO WHOM HONOUR IS DUE.

WE were now making preparations for the funeral of young Schmidt. At the burial of poor Nel, the body was simply wrapped in cotton blankets and lowered into the grave; it was a painful sight, and we were anxious not to have a repetition of it. In the company of Lieutenant Holzer, I proceeded to the artillery camp to make arrangements; there we found Mr. Veyleveldt making a coffin out of some packing cases. After searching through the camp, I found some sheeting, and this, together with a few cotton blankets, served to line the rude encasement. The body, which was lying close to my wagon, was placed in it, and a procession formed. The first part of the service I read under our bucksail; we then walked to the grave, which had been dug next to that of Nel. Mr. Schmidt, already referred to as having fallen into Nel's grave, and who had now quite recovered, was present as chief mourner, he being a relative of the deceased. Immediately after the service, at a signal from Sergeant Charles Lever, three volleys were fired by a firing party, consisting of Sergeant Charles Lever (in charge), B. Yorke, Acton, Smit, Ramsay, Scobel, and Emmenes, these being present when poor Schmidt was fatally wounded. The coffin was covered with the vierkleur, and strewn with maidenhair ferns and wild flowers. Great credit was due to Lieutenant Holzer for carrying out the funeral arrangements with such regard for decency and order.

Referring to the incident of the fight I have already described, the highest praise is due to Willie Keith, for the coolness he displayed when things were looking very critical. He was walking between Dunsdon and Cowley, when each of his companions were shot down, and Schmidt shot just in advance of him. He and George Scobel then covered the wounded men with their own bodies, until assistance came. A word is also due to Ramsay and Bertie Yorke, who, at great personal risk, rendered medical assistance to the injured, and helped to get them into safety. It was incidents of this description that proved the pluck and *esprit de corps* of the Pretorians, and they were not forgotten by their fellow-townsmen on their return to the capital.

Much criticism had taken place on the military manœuvres of those who were risking their lives, not only for the safety of the country, but also for white prestige in South Africa. It mattered little what the rights or wrongs of the case were, for when once at war with the natives, every white man should know that his very existence in South Africa depends on victory for his side. Once let the natives get the idea that they can beat the whites in open war, and chaos will ensue. The blacks number about ten times as many as the whites; but, though the latter are numerically so inferior, yet it is only natural that they should take the lead. Enlightenment and civilisation must rule, and it is absolutely necessary for the safety and progress of the country that the native races should be subdued and compelled to submit to the laws of the land, instead of being governed by their own petty autocratic chiefs, who are a great hindrance to the proper development of the country. Therefore, when disputes have to be settled by the fierce arbitrament of war, then especially must the result not hang in the balance.

But instead of encouraging the men who were doing their duty bravely and gratuitously at the front, all kinds of charges appeared in the press: as, for instance, the use of dynamite was deprecated, notwithstanding the great successes our own people (British) have achieved with this and similar means in their Kafir wars. Yet Englishmen, forgetting these facts, would have prevented the General from speedily terminating the war by the use of dynamite. How anyone can discriminate between the use of dynamite and hand grenades or explosive shells, passes my comprehension. Then the chivalry of General Joubert, unparalleled in South African warfare, in offering the native women and children an opportunity to escape, met with no comment whatever. After what had been said and written with regard to the General's conduct, it would have been only just to have recognised such a merciful act, and, indeed it should have been recognised by all humane men; but far from meeting with notice, it was slurred over, and columns of leaded type set forth the fact, that while the flag of truce was flying the Boers prevented the enemy from taking advantage of the flag, raised to enable him to send out his women and children to drink.

But again no notice was taken of the enemy, under cover of this flag, treacherously striving to better his position, by shifting his men and grazing his goats.

Again, a few days previous, whilst another flag of truce was flying, we found the enemy sending water carriers to get in a supply of water, so as to enable him to hold out; but the Boers stayed their hands, with the result that a score or more of brave men were lying either dead or wounded.

The presence of Mrs. Joubert, too, at the front was heroic, and also an unusual feature in South African warfare; whilst the list of dead and wounded told its own tale; the majority of whom were those of our Dutch countrymen, men who, like others, have their faults, but who have also a record for personal bravery equal to that of any modern nation. It is the fashion to decry the Boer, but those who had personal experience of the events of 1881, know the men, who dared the might of Great Britain, and who are by no means as bad as represented. We are not imbued with a favourable opinion of the Boer; as a legislator we know he is full of faults, and we lose no opportunity in pointing them out; it is therefore only fair to show up their good qualities in the most favourable light, when we can do so honestly and truthfully, more especially as they must some day be our fellow-citizens.

A krijsraad was held at Vorster's kopje, and amongst other things discussed was the advisability of burning the bush down with the aid of paraffin, a suggestion made by Commandant Malan.

The sequel to the big fire which was seen on Fort Jonker kopje and the discovery of the spoor of a large number of natives, was that they were some of Kiviet's Kafirs, as they were known to have had two horses with them.

The General ordered the Marico contingent to complete the fort commenced by the Pretorians, but they distinctly refused to do so, saying that they had already built one fort and lost men in doing so, and had manned another, and did not see why they should be called upon to do work which appeared to be essentially the duty of Vorster's commando.

Their excuse was apparently deemed sufficient, for the General made no attempt to enforce his order.

This circumstance, amounting to mutiny, placed the General in an awkward position. It proved the truth of the proverb of bringing a horse to the water, but the impossibility of making him drink. The Marico men played the part of the horse, the water is well exemplified by the fort to be built, overlooking a running stream. But even the General's own orders would not make the horse drink, nor prevent his kicking.

It seems almost incredible that the orders of a General to his men on active service could be flouted with impunity! The title of "General" on such an expedition was simply an anomaly. Had Volunteers been called out instead of the "loyal" burgher being forced into action, and had the Hoofdstad been stormed sooner instead of so much time wasted in scheming and dilly-dallying, fewer lives would probably have been lost, and the war brought to a speedier termination.

The position of the General was, to say the least of it, most trying, and, taking all things into consideration, he could not have acted better than he did; he displayed great tact and patience combined with mercy, and his actions are deserving of the highest praise.

Yesterday, whilst a friendly native was going up the mountain from the Middelburg laager with provisions, he received a wound in the arm which necessitated amputation. After the operation had been performed, it was found that the missile was a stone, about the size of a man's thumb, which shattered the bone and splintered itself. He was less than one thousand yards from the laager when he was shot. This proved the presence of the enemy in that part of the mountain.

A grave scandal arose owing to the inadequate arrangements made for the herding and protection of the captured cattle, of which a large number was missing; by whom they had been removed was a matter of doubt, but it was a fact that of the total number taken, scarcely a thousand remained. Two "*boys*" were seen driving a small troop off in the direction of Pietersburg, and mounted men went in pursuit. A native, who represented himself as one of Malitse's men, was captured in close proximity to the camp, and from the unsatisfactory nature of his replies, as well as that a quantity of stone bullets were found upon him, he was suspected of being a spy, and taken to the General to be dealt with.

DR. JAMESON.

ACTING VELD-CORNET CHARLES RICE.

[*To face page* 145.

CHAPTER XXIII.

THE CHIEF MEDICAL OFFICER.

ON Monday, the 16th July, Colonel Ferreira left for Pietersburg *en route* to Pretoria. Lieutenant Rice was appointed Acting Veld-Cornet during his absence; Lieutenant Holzer being in charge of the laager.

In coming down the mountain the Colonel and his party were fired on from about twenty different places.

Although I did not wish to be a pessimist or an alarmist, I could not help viewing the conduct of the campaign with serious misgiving.

Had a determined attempt been made when we first advanced towards the Hoofdstad to storm the caves with our full strength, I believe that the enemy, being then apparently in a state of fear, would have been easily overcome, and the war brought to an end at once; but the delay had given the enemy an amount of confidence which he never possessed before, and instead of retreating as heretofore, he had assumed the offensive with considerable success.

Fort Pretoria was situated two thousand seven hundred feet above the laager, and was distant some seven and a half miles; yet for the whole distance there was no protection for those bringing up supplies, beyond twenty-five men at Fort Jonker, which was fifteen hundred yards from the path, and about thirty friendly Kafirs at a point some two miles further on. Moreover, the only means at first of obtaining supplies on the top of the mountain was by Kafir bearers, as the mountain was too steep for the wagons to go further than the base.

Two men of the Pretoria contingent, Messrs. Watkins and Claridge, were afterwards told off by Colonel Ferreira to supervise the transport; using pack-horses for the purpose, they ascended the mountain every day between 3 and 4 A.M., returning at about 2 P.M.

With regard to the laager itself, it was thought owing to its size, nature and position, that at least five hundred men would be required to effectually defend it; and as most of our men were always on the mountain, matters would have been very serious had Malaboch taken it into his head to create a diversion by paying it a visit. This was thought to be highly improbable; but, nevertheless, many a sleepless night I spent in thinking of the possibility of such an event.

D. Prinsloo, of the Zoutpansberg commando, was shot when coming down the mountain. His son had only that day arrived to act as his substitute, and Prinsloo, having bade good-bye to his friends, was proceeding towards Mapen's when four shots from each side of the path were fired at him; only one struck him, this passing through his groin, but did not stop his progress. At a further point he was fired at again, but was not hit. The Kafirs, however, followed the blood stains, thinking that as he was wounded he would soon fall. Luckily some Zoutpansbergers, who happened to be going up to the fort; met him, but although they saw the Kafirs they did not fire on them, believing they were some of our native allies.

This fatal confusion of friendlies and enemies was indirectly the cause of our loss during the last engagement, as when our people in Fort Pretoria saw Kafirs coming up in the rear of the detachment they did not fire, thinking they were some of Commandant Vorster's "*boys.*" It was a great pity that steps had not been taken to give our allies some distinctive dress, by which they might have been at once recognised.

They had had provided for them red and white ribands to put round their heads; but, as can be easily understood, this was not sufficient, as Malaboch's natives could have easily worn such a badge. This oversight was, however, only on a par with many others which had characterised the progress of the expedition ever since it was promulgated—I cannot say organised—there had been little enough of organisation all through the proceedings.

Heavy firing was heard in the direction of the Middelburg fort, and I learned afterwards that while three men were going through the bush, the Kafirs attacked them, and one, named Piet Goosen, was shot through the shoulder. The men in the fort fired several volleys and the enemy retreated.

News reached us that our native allies managed to surprise a number of the enemy sitting outside a cave ; they killed ten of them before they could take refuge. When they had taken cover the enemy replied to the fire, killing one native ally and wounding two others.

On Thursday, the 19th July, Dr. Laxton arrived in camp, and was attached to the Medical Corps, help being much needed in that department. I visited poor Lottering to-day and found him in a dying state ; the doctor, as a last resource, had amputated the arm, so as to do everything possible in order to save his life, but it was a hopeless case from the beginning : mortification had set in long before the operation was performed. The poor fellow was unable to speak, although quite conscious ; by signs he asked for water, and by the same means made me understand that he knew he was dying. He expired soon after I left, and was buried in the artillery camp the same day by the Rev. Mr. Burgers, a minister of the Dutch Reformed Church, who was up on a visit from Middelburg. Three volleys were fired over the grave at the conclusion of the service.

In pursuance of our endeavour to effectually cut off the enemy's water supply, it was found necessary to construct another small fort immediately opposite the Hoofdstad, at a spot not more than two hundred and fifty yards therefrom.

This was satisfactorily accomplished, and a party

of the Middelburgers was told off to hold the position. During the construction of the fort the enemy kept up a smart fire, and a man named Leclercq received a bullet which completely smashed his left thigh, shattering the bone, and necessitating amputation; two others sustaining slight wounds. Information of these casualties was received through the heliograph, and Mr. F. Neel ascended the mountain at 5 P.M. for the purpose of bringing Leclercq down; he returned with his charge at 11 P.M., and placed him in hospital.

A stalwart Kafir was shot by our men a few days ago; when picked up he was found to be armed with a Snider rifle, but he wore a bandolier containing one hundred Martini cartridges. These had been clinked in a peculiar manner so as to fit the rifle; a fact which spoke volumes for the ingenuity of the enemy. He was dressed in European clothes, and was believed to be one of Malaboch's chief indunas.

The natives in the caves displayed a white flag, but it was immediately shot down. The General now rescinded his previous order of not regarding a flag of truce, and for the future it was to be respected. A few days after this incident the enemy began sounding their horns, and shortly afterwards one of them made his appearance at the mouth of the cave with a flag of truce; scarcely, however, had he done so, than it was simply riddled with bullets. On the same day two of the enemy were shot, one being killed and the other wounded. Not long afterwards another flag was displayed at the entrance to the enemy's stronghold, but warned by previous experience, they did not themselves show up. This, however, did not save the flag, which was promptly shot away.

Incidents such as the foregoing were the more regrettable from the fact that very strict orders had been given by the General, who now expressed his intention of making it his especial business to severely punish any man guilty of such flagrant violation of regulations.

The whole of the Pretoria contingent was now ordered up the mountain, as the storming of the caves was anticipated the following day. Captain Shiel's Knobneusen had arrived, and were also to take part in the attack. A sortie was made from the Middelburg fort, a number of Kafirs being observed in the bush; a skirmish ensued, with the result that ten of the enemy were killed and one of our friendlies wounded.

Henry Leclercq, whom I visited while Lottering was lying dead in his tent, asked me how he (Lottering) was. I replied that he was no better. He begged of me to visit him again soon; the amputation of the leg was to take place the following day. The operation was most cleverly performed by Dr. Mader in the presence of Drs. Laxton and Liknaitzky, Messrs. Neel, Lever and Brook rendering assistance. The patient was exceedingly weak and caused the doctor much anxiety. The amputation had been delayed in order to allow Dr. Hohls, of Pietersburg, to be present. All this time (some days) Dr. Mader was kept in the greatest suspense and anxiety, as the patient's friends would not consent to the amputation before Dr. Hohls had been consulted.

After the doctor's decision to amputate had been made known, the Rev. Mr. Burgers asked if the limb could not really be saved. The doctor replied that he could only save the leg at the cost of the patient's life, and that, even after amputation, he could hold out little or no hopes of saving his life, owing to the unfortunate delay. As I have mentioned in a previous chapter, the doctor's opinions were never regarded nor his advice accepted among the Boers; and amputation was almost in every case postponed until it was too late to do any good.

It was the general verdict among the doctors and others who rendered assistance at the various operations, that the chief medical officer was a gentleman of undoubted ability in his profession, an exceptionally clever surgeon, and one who always performed his work in an expeditious and skilful manner.

The next morning, on my way to visit the wounded, I saw about two thousand friendly Kafirs, sent by the Chief Malitse for the purpose of skirmishing and clearing the mountain of the enemy. They were distinguished from Mathala's Kafirs by a white band on their heads.

I found poor Leclercq delirious, and was pained when I observed the anxiety on the face of the tender-hearted doctor, who was most kind and sympathetic, and naturally much interested in his case. As he said himself, "I would do anything that would help towards saving the life of my patient." He was present with me during my brief stay, and that was the last time I saw Leclercq, for he died that evening. On leaving Leclercq's tent, the doctor informed me that it would be necessary to amputate Van der Westhuizen's arm, as the bones were completely smashed. The bullet had entered the arm below the elbow, passing through the bone above the joint. The next morning I witnessed the operation performed by Dr. Mader, who was assisted by Drs. Laxton, Liknaitzky, and Mr. Fred Neel, Dr. Laxton administering the chloroform. The patient lost very little blood, the whole thing only occupying thirty-five minutes. In the evening I heard of the critical condition of Leclercq, and while on my way with Dr. Liknaitzky to visit him, he expired. He was buried next day with military honours, the Commandant-General being present at the funeral.

The Kafirs now turned the tables by taking to the offensive, and the Pretorians were the recipients of the attack; they (the Pretorians) occupied a fort situated on a ledge about three hundred yards lower than Fort Pretoria, and immediately overlooking the scene of the last engagement. Owing to the bitterly cold weather, most of the men had selected sheltered nooks among the boulders within a short distance of the fort and inside the line of pickets. The fact that the Kafirs had kept decidedly in the background during the last few days caused the men to get a little careless, and instead of extinguishing all fires at sundown and retiring to shelter, they gathered in social groups round the cheery camp-fires until long after that time. At about half-past seven, after Lieutenant Schroeder and Sergeant Jan Lourens had just finished their rounds, and everything appeared quiet and safe, the men were suddenly roused by two startling volleys of bullets being poured in upon them. Under cover of darkness and the uneven scrubby boulders, a body of the enemy had advanced in crescent shape from behind, to within twenty or thirty yards of the pickets, and then commenced firing upon the groups gathered round the fires. Bullets fell thickly all round, and could be distinctly heard as they struck the boulders; fortunately only two men were injured. One was Barend Nel, who was standing with his hands in his overcoat pockets. A bullet passed through his right hand, damaging it very severely, while his overcoat was perforated in two other places, luckily without doing him further injury. The other victim, Marthynus van Vuren, who formed one of a group nearest the line of pickets, was shot through the right thigh, the bullet passing between the large vein and the bone. An order had been given, that in the event of surprise, the men were to retire within the precincts of the fort before returning the enemy's fire. As soon, therefore, as the volleys were heard, a rush was made for the fort; the men stumbled over the uneven ground in the hurried scamper, but the fort was reached in safety with no further casualties. The walls were immediately manned, and strengthened with logs of wood that were lying inside, and then a regular fusilade of bullets was poured upon the position presumed to be occupied by the Kafirs, while hand-grenades were thrown into the crevices and fissures which surrounded the fort. Our fire was not returned, but meanwhile the position was a precarious one; and until the moon rose, about 9.30, our men had an anxious time. Then a sortie was made to bring in the blankets and anything else that might have been left outside, and also to ascertain if the enemy was in the neighbourhood; without interference the Pretorians succeeded in bringing in everything. Some anxiety was caused on the calling of the roll, by the absence of five men; but on a reconnoitring party going in search of them, it was found they were lying low in a deep recess from which they were brought to the fort unscathed. The remainder of the night was passed in quietude, every attention being given to the wounded; and Messrs. W. R. Ramsay and F. B. Tobias (LL.D.), who were possessed of some surgical knowledge, should be especially mentioned in this connection. It was indeed a matter of extreme regret that there were no medical officers nearer than the laager, several miles away; and even what little there was in the way of bandages and lint had been removed the day before, so that Nel's and Van Vuren's wounds had to be bound up with torn handkerchiefs obtained from their comrades. In the morning a picket was sent out to patrol the vicinity of the fort; the place was found to be perfectly clear, but the enemy had approached to within thirty yards of the fort. Empty cartridge cases, different to those served out to our forces, were picked up, many of them being Ely's. Under escort, the wounded were conveyed to the hospital in safety. It was found, on examination by Dr. Liknaitzky, that Nel's second finger was smashed just below the knuckle joint, and that it would have to be taken off. Immediately on the news of the attack becoming known in the Pretoria laager fifty men were ordered to proceed to the assistance of their comrades in the fort; and although the majority of them had only come down from the mountain a day or two before, after a long spell, they obeyed the order, much to their credit, without a murmur, seemingly pleased at the idea of being in the thick of it again.

CHAPTER XXIV.

THE TERRIBLE DEATH OF GROENEWALD—MR. FRED NEEL MEETS WITH AN ACCIDENT.

SEVERAL Boers from the Waterberg laager sallied out to set fire to some of the huts in the Hoofdstad. They had succeeded in their object, and were about to retire, when one of their number, L. Groenewald by name, saw a beehive on a rock above him, and stated his determination to take it back with him, despite the warnings of his companions. In order to effect his purpose, he laid his gun down, and raised himself on to the ledge. Scarcely had he done this, when he was shot through the heart, and fell back into the flames of the burning huts. To rescue him at once was an impossibility, as the cartridges in his bandolier began exploding one after the other; but as soon as they were able to approach the spot, Clark, a young Englishman, and some others, dashed in to get the body out, under cover of a heavy fire from the forts. On reaching the spot where he had fallen, a gruesome sight met their gaze, for in place of Groenewald, there were only his charred remains. Great regret was expressed in the Pretoria laager at his sad fate, as he had been particularly kind to our wounded while they were being brought down the mountain on the occasion of the fight at the water.

Two hundred and fifty Kafirs, under command of G. W. Burnett and five others of the Pretoria contingent, left the camp on the morning of the 24th July, taking the south face of the mountain, and reached Fort Pretoria without check. On their way they passed two large caves, which, though deserted, bore traces of recent occupation. They also saw the corpse of an old man who had evidently died of starvation. The next morning, at daybreak, they commenced to scour the dense bush, which extended from immediately below Fort Ferreira to the opposite range, at the rear of the artillery fort, the party being augmented by two artillerymen, bringing the total number of Europeans up to eight. Their names were, G. W. Burnett, N. Vlok, W. J. Hornebrook, J. Nell, J. Conroy, D. Coetzee, and Corporals W. Davitt and Versity. They advanced in skirmishing order, and when they reached the spot where the Pretorians were attacked, they were fired upon from the Hoofdstad, and Burnett fell wounded in the right shoulder. Almost at the same time, one of the friendly Kafirs was shot, whereupon the whole native contingent, with the exception of about a dozen, bolted off, leaving the whites to shift for themselves. J. Nell ran back, with the idea of rallying his natives, whilst the rest of the party assisted Burnett and the wounded Kafir to the artillery fort. Nell was missing for a long time, and grave fears were entertained for his safety, but he eventually returned to camp. A message was at once heliographed to Fort Pretoria for medical assistance, and Dr. Laxton, escorted by Lieutenant Schroeder and seventeen men, was speedily in attendance. The escort party, together with some fifty or sixty friendly Kafirs, who had been rallied, then received orders to build a fort, some two hundred and fifty yards from the Hoofdstad. This they successfully accomplished, and, in addition, erected two smaller forts, which formed a chain to the foot of the krantz, and thus effectually cut off the enemy's water supply. During the erection of these forts our men came across the dead bodies of two of the enemy, no doubt shot in the previous engagement. At the moment Burnett fell, some twenty or more of the enemy fled out of the bush in the direction of the cave, and in crossing the open, ten of them were shot, and a shell from the mountain-gun dispersed the remainder. It was beyond doubt that the enemy had quite recently received supplies of first-class rifles and ammunition.

Incredible as it seemed, many of them were well armed with Express rifles, and that they knew how to use them was painfully evident, whilst the quality of their ammunition was sufficiently vouched for by their empty cartridge-cases, which bore the well-known name of Ely Brothers.

Whereas, in our first advance, the muzzle-loader was very much in evidence, and the dull boom of the elephant gun easily recognisable, it was a noticeable fact that, in later encounters, the sharp ping of the Express was the only sound distinguishable.

Dr. Mader, the Government medical officer, handed in his resignation on the 26th July, owing to unwarrantable interference with him in his professional capacity. Without giving him the slightest notice, one of his patients, Goosen by name, was removed from hospital, and afterwards attended to by Mesdames Joubert and Vorster.

Mr. Fred Neel, whilst returning to camp, after visiting one of the other laagers, met with a nasty accident which might easily have been attended with fatal consequences. His horse suddenly became restive, the saddle-girths snapped, and he was thrown heavily to the ground, severely spraining his wrist and arm, and sustaining slight concussion of the brain.

Arrangements were being made for the storming of the Hoofdstad, but it was thought that, even if successful in this endeavour, it would not mean the termination of the campaign, as the general impression was that Malaboch and his warriors had fled from the cave. On the other hand, we were convinced that the Chief would make a desperate stand on the back mountain, and that a determined attack would yet remain to be made in that direction. The possibility of the slaughter of one hundred natives in the caves adjoining the stad would not mean the slaughter of Malaboch. There had been too much dilly-dallying. The General, although a capable commander, owing to his thorough knowledge of the Kafir character and their war tactics, was, in my opinion, too much of a *dilettante*; for had a bold attack been made when we first arrived, matters would have been brought to an issue long ago, and without much loss of life.

CHAPTER XXV.

A COURT-MARTIAL.

ON Friday, July 29th, a court-martial was held for the trial of a prisoner named George Nefdt. At 10 o'clock punctually, members of the court took their seats; Commandant Vorster presided, and the other members were Commandants Grobler and Botha, Veld-Cornets Botha, Louw, Burgers, Kleinenburg, and Van Dyk.

Dr. Tobias opened by stating the case for the prosecution, and the indictment of the prisoner was as follows :—

"Before the Krijsraad in session in small or ordinary court-martial on Maloboch's Commando, on the matter of the Krijsraad before mentioned *vs.* George Nefdt.

"Dr. Frederic Balthazer Tobias, who prosecutes on behalf of the Krijsraad, hereby notifies that in consequence of information which was furnished him by Colonel Ignatius Ferreira, and as such serving on the Malaboch Commando, a certain white person, named George Nefdt, of Pretoria, serving as a substitute for a properly commandeered person, and at present a prisoner in the artillery camp at Blaauwberg, is guilty of drunkenness and insubordination, which is a punishable offence according to Article 27 of Act No. 2 of 1883 :

"He, the said George Nefdt, having on or about the 8th July, 1894, in the camp Laager No. 2 at Blaauwberg, of the Pretoria District Burghers, under Commandant D. J. E. Erasmus; and,

A COURT-MARTIAL

furthermore, consecutively on the 9th, 10th, 11th and 12th July, 1894, in the Fort Pretoria near the Hoofdstad of Malaboch, while in a state of intoxication, and in the presence of several Veld-Cornets and Commandants, did utter, in a loud tone of voice, all kinds of insulting expressions and rebellious remarks, especially vilifying his acting serving Veld-Cornet, the said Colonel Ferreira, who was present in the said fort, such as the following: That Colonel Ferreira is drunk daily and lies amongst the boulders with a bottle of whisky; that Colonel Ferreira had sent away numbers of goats and oxen with a letter whereon there was no address; that Colonel Ferreira with the English and the Hollanders consumed the provisions which had been sent up from Pretoria for the use of everybody, amongst which were milk, whisky, gin, corned beef, jam, and other articles, which had disappeared without a trace; and that in a loud tone of voice Nefdt had accused Colonel Ferreira of having stolen these articles and robbed the Burghers of the Commando; or to have used words to that effect, or of a similar tendency, and that he, the said Nefdt, had also challenged Colonel Ferreira to fight with him, for which reasons Dr. F. B. Tobias, before mentioned, submits that the said George Nefdt, after having been examined and found guilty, shall be dealt with according to the law! Dr. F. B. Tobias for the prosecution, Artillery Camp at Blaauwberg, 16th July, 1894."

At the termination of the reading of the charge Captain Schiel, who was defending the prisoner, requested permission to question the constitution of the court, pointing out that, according to the laws governing all courts-martial in the world, the prisoner had a right to object to any member of the court, exactly as in a civil court an objection to a juryman is allowed. The learned advocate for the prosecution, however, pointed out that the court was not a court-martial in the strict military sense of the word, but rather a court standing alone, being the outcome of a military system peculiar to this country, and that the court was not a jury, but a court having the rights of the judges in a civil court. The President inquired who it was to whom the prisoner objected, and why?

Veld-Cornet Botha was named by Captain Schiel, on account of his already having expressed his intention of giving the prisoner three years' hard labour and twenty-five lashes. Veld-Cornet Botha rose excitedly, and gave the lie direct to Captain Schiel, amidst the expressed disapproval of his colleagues. Captain Schiel did not attempt to press the truth of the reason given, but claimed his right to object to the Veld-Cornet without giving any reason. In spite of the admitted practice of the world, the court refused Captain Schiel's request.

Nothing daunted at losing his first point, the Captain opened fire a second time, and inquired whether Colonel Ferreira had been subpœnaed and would appear. On being answered in the negative, he stated that his defence mainly rested on cross-examination of the complainant; he appeared at the court to give the prisoner every opportunity. "Where was the Colonel? Why did he go to Pietpotgieters Rust?" The learned advocate on his side did not see any need for the presence of Colonel Ferreira; the charge was drunkenness and insubordination, and the complainant was the Government, and no particular man. The court was of opinion that the case should be adjourned until the return of the absent Colonel. Captain Schiel immediately rose and objected—the prisoner had already been some time under arrest, and to postpone the case further would be against the law. The President wished to inquire of the learned advocate as to the law on the point. Dr. Tobias stated that the presence of the Colonel was not necessary, but that, if the court held that Ferreira's presence was necessary, it would be against the law to postpone the case further. The court being convinced by the Captain, dismissed the case, thus practically giving a verdict for the prisoner. The decision was received with applause. Outside, three cheers were raised by some of the Pretoria people for Captain Schiel, and he was carried on the shoulders of the crowd.

Without doubt, Schiel's speech carried not only the court but the public with it, and he was to be congratulated for his spirited defence of an unfortunate Uitlander, whose worst crime was, not looking upon the wine when it was red, but partaking, not wisely, though too freely, of the whisky.

CHAPTER XXVI.

ACCIDENT TO CAPTAIN STENT—THE COMMISSARY-GENERAL.

July 27.—This morning, the enemy created a further diversion by attacking the artillery fort. The first indication of their presence was received a little after seven o'clock in the shape of a withering fire from the surrounding bush, at a distance of about three hundred yards. Until this moment, the friendly Kafirs, who were occupying the fort, had believed themselves to be in perfect safety; but no sooner had the ping, ping, and plash of the bullets against the stone walls afforded them an unpleasant surprise, than a panic seemed to have set in amongst them, and they left the fort to take care of itself. There was a regular rush to seek shelter in the bush, only twelve men, in addition to the artillerymen, retaining their presence of mind. They had the greatest possible difficulty in dragging the gun round, so as to train it on to the enemy's position, and were subjected the whole time to a steady fire, which, although well directed, fortunately failed in effect. Several shells were placed in the bush where it was thought the bulk of the enemy was, and they had the effect of forcing the Kafirs to retire.

After two hours of warm firing, in which no one was hurt on our side, the enemy went further back, but still continued to keep up desultory fire, which considerably hampered the movements of those in the fort, as our men were watching an opportunity to return to the camp.

I have mentioned that the fire was desultory, but there was a peculiarity about the accuracy of the firing, observed by a few who had to go from fort to fort, also about the class of ammunition used, and inferentially, the kind of arms; for those used on this occasion by Maloboch's people were undoubtedly muzzle-loaders, whereas it was practically certain that all the Kafirs left in the Hoofdstad were armed with Sniders, Martinis, and Empress rifles. Reinforcements must have evidently arrived for Maloboch, but from which direction they came in it was difficult to say.

Captain Stent met with a slight mishap to-day whilst firing his revolver. He was coming down the mountain with Dr. Laxton, and emptied his weapon in the direction of a cave, when by some mischance he received a wound in the forehead, which, however, was not serious.

Two pumping engines arrived to-day for the purpose of spraying the bush with paraffin.

Mr. Meyer, the Chief Commissariat Officer, spared no pains in creating a very bitter feeling between the Uitlanders and the Boers; and it was perhaps only the respect which the Pretorians had for their own officers and the General that prevented a very serious outbreak. I have already mentioned the fact that whilst other laagers had been supplied with clothing and other necessaries, the Pretoria men had been sent from pillar to post, and whilst about half of them had received a partial supply, the others had still to remain without shoes and other equipment.

Dr. Laxton, on first seeing the men on the mountain, dubbed them " The Ragged Brigade."

It was acknowledged on all sides they had done the lion's share of the work ; had taken risks which no other contingent would incur ; had been drafted out for the use of other laagers, and although numbering only one hundred and seventy-five all told, they had experienced more casualties than any other contingent. The whole of the hospital staff had been selected from the Pretoria detachment ; yet in the face of all this the commissariat officer had the audacity to tell Lieutenant Holzer (in my hearing), on his presenting a requisition, signed by the Acting Commandant-General, for the men's clothing, that he was not going to give them, and that the Pretorians " were a lot of d—— scoundrels, trying to defraud the Government."

In addition to this, he refused to issue anything to the wounded men unless they paraded before him. And the result was, that Van de Westhuizen, who had only had his arm amputated a few days previously, had to walk about six hundred yards, clad only in a blanket; Dunsdon, with a borrowed overcoat but no trousers ; Loveday, in borrowed clothing ; and Cowley, in his own blood-bespattered garments. Mr. Austin

Brook, who had voluntarily joined himself to the hospital staff, and was devoting his whole time and energy to the care of the wounded (not by any means an easy or pleasant task), tried his utmost to prevent the wounded men taking this journey; but his repeated applications to Mr. Meyer were of no avail, although he produced a requisition properly signed. The answer given was, that if the wounded men were too ill to get up and walk, then clothes would be of no use to them. So all had to undertake this journey, although weak to a degree from the effects of their wounds. Others were commonly informed that they would have nothing, as they did not appear in person. Referring to the wounded Kafirs, he wanted to know what good clothes and blankets were to them. It was a great pity that such conduct passed unrebuked. Of this I am certain, that these things were not done with the knowledge of the General or the Government, who would have rectified them at once had they known the true state of affairs.

CHAPTER XXVII.

NEARING THE END—SURRENDER OF WOMEN AND CHILDREN—MALABOCH SPEAKS.

THE war now underwent a fresh phase—over a hundred women and children came out from various caves close to the Hoofdstad and gave themselves up. They were suffering terribly from the pangs of thirst, and it was truly a pitiful sight to see the unfortunate youngsters crawling along the ground to get hold of anything that looked like a calabash containing water, so as to relieve their parched mouths. Young and old had to be dragged forcibly away from the water, otherwise they would have drunk themselves to death. At 5 o'clock in the evening the General issued an order that twenty men from the Pretoria contingent, and a similar number of Boers, were to go with the friendly natives, numbering over five hundred, and surround the big cave, so as to prevent the enemy coming out to fetch water. The movement was entirely successful. Our people approaching to within seventy yards of the caves, and standing about three yards from one another, effectually hemmed Malaboch's people in, whilst every man in each of the six forts which now guarded the water and the flats stood to arms to render assistance

MALABOCH AT BAY.

To face page 169.

if necessary. At 9.30 a number of the enemy sallied out with the idea of obtaining water, and knowing the position our men had taken up, fired several shots in that direction. This was accepted as a signal for a return fire of gigantic dimensions, and the reader can imagine what it was like when I mention that nearly six hundred rifles were fired simultaneously, and that the firing line spread over about three quarters of a mile. The interchange of shots was kept up for about ten minutes, no one on our side being injured, but one of the enemy was wounded in the leg, and ultimately committed suicide; as when his body was found the next morning, it was seen that he had placed the barrel of his rifle in his mouth, and had blown the top of his head off.

A cessation of hostilities was brought about by our people hearing a clear manly voice ring out in stentorian tones from a rock close to the stad. It was a dark night, and therefore impossible to obtain even a glimpse of the speaker, but the musical notes and distinctness of utterance carried with them their own impress of dignity, and everybody knew that it was Malaboch himself who was addressing them. What a voice it was that hushed the strife and commanded attention can be understood from the fact that it penetrated the forts behind, fully two hundred and fifty yards away, and each word was eagerly listened to as it fell from the Chief's lips, and thus it was he spoke :

" You have taken from me my women and children, my cattle and corn; my villages have you burned, and now you will not even let me have a drink of water; everything that was mine you have, wait until to-morrow and you shall have me. What do you seek in fighting to-night?"

And he who was interpreting replied: "The wolves and jackals come out from their holes only when darkness has covered the land, so they must be hunted during the night. Come forth in the light of day, and we will hear what you have to say; but if you will not face the sun, then we must shoot you as we shoot the jackals."

Malaboch's response was anxiously awaited, but none was forthcoming, save an abrupt request that he might be allowed to see Mr. Sonntag, the missionary. The rest of the night was spent in silence, though sleep was not permitted.

At an early hour the next morning the reverend gentleman went up to the cave, and shortly after his entrance sounds as of singing were heard. A long palaver then evidently took place, but of what nature I am unable to say.

The next incident, however, was a shout from the stad, asking our men to refrain from firing, as the rest of the women and children and old men were coming out, and immediately after, out they trooped. Nobody who witnessed the scene—alas, for the horrors of war—is likely soon to forget it! Most of the unfortunate creatures showed visible signs of exhaustion, and some of the old women, white-haired and decrepit, were so enfeebled by age that they had to be carried on the backs of the maidens. Wounded

Kafirs of both sexes were borne along in the throng, and one old woman struggled desperately down the path with a ghastly burden on her shoulders. At first it could not be quite discerned what it was she was carrying, but on her nearer approach, it proved to be a young warrior, her son. He had been shot just above the ankle, and the leg, having rotted right away up to the thigh, emitted a most fearful stench. Terrible tales were told by the natives who had given themselves up; they said there were scores of dead bodies in the cave, and that they were piled up at the entrance so as to prevent the shells bursting inside. The sufferings of the wounded must have been too dreadful for words, for in almost every case mortification had set in. Many women, it appeared, had been shot in their attempts to reach the water, the majority being wounded in the feet or lower portion of their limbs.

At midday the missionary came out of the caves accompanied by Malaboch's brother, who wished to surrender. The latter brought the General a present of a sum of money in gold from the Chief; but the General declined to accept it, and told the bearer to return and tell Malaboch that he must give himself up before sunset, and those of his people who did not wish to be killed were to come out without delay. The mission did not appear to be a very palatable one to the brother, but on being assured that he would not be fired upon by our men, he went in and delivered the message, and afterwards returned to our lines.

Altogether four hundred and ninety-three people had surrendered since yesterday, but none amongst these were young bloods, and very few appeared to have come from the cave itself. Malaboch's one hope consisted in being able to break through our chain of forts, and connect with his forces on the back of the mountain. To prevent this the General strained every nerve; for he is said to have remarked, that unless we "*scotch*" Malaboch now, we shall have a guerilla war more troublesome than any yet experienced in South Africa.

The next morning, Sunday, the 29th of July, news reached us that Malaboch had expressed his intention to come out during the day, and the white flag was flying. There was a report that Malaboch had been wounded, but there was no truth in the rumour; and most of us would have been sorry if the Chief had been either killed or wounded. A man who, with less than a thousand Kafirs (I do not think there were more), had kept about two thousand white men at bay for two months, was worthy of admiration.

CHAPTER XXVIII.

A NIGHT ON THE MOUNTAIN IN THE MOONLIGHT—
MR. JENKINS' PICNIC PARTY.

A FEW days prior to Malaboch's surrender, Captain Stent spent a night upon the mountain. The following is his description of the time so spent. It was, to say the least of it, exciting:—

"The first part of the night was dark as pitch, save where the dull gleam of the dying bivouac fires shone on the stone walls of the fort, making darkness visible. Now and again, from the cliffs opposite, a gleam of light would be followed by the flash and roar of a hand-grenade, and the whole mountain side would echo and re-echo until the sound died away in a hoarse whispering murmur from some distant forest. No sooner did silence reign again, than a rattling volley came from a picket, where some poor thirsty wretch was running a last desperate risk in the hope of obtaining a mouthful of cold water. At midnight the moon rose cold and majestic, tinging first the eastern sky with its glow, then touching peak after peak and krantz after krantz, until at last it glistened on the water in the ravine below us, and the whole scene was bathed in the soft mellow light. In the forts could be seen the glint of rifle barrels, and the dark forms of sentries on the ramparts, alert to catch the slightest sound that might betray a hidden foe, while in the beleaguered town lights moved to and fro, and, stealthily, naked forms crept from hut to hut. All night long we watched and waited until the grey dawn released each sentry from his post, and the fires crackled merrily under the early coffee-kettle. Men threw off their blankets, and the dull boom of a distant cannon greeted the rising sun.

"Soon after sunrise, on Thursday the 26th July, I started to have a look at the Pretoria Johnnies, and had got some three hundred yards from the fort, accompanied by one man, when the enemy suddenly opened fire from the rear, entirely outside the circle of forts. My companion's opinion was that we had better get back within the fort as rapidly as possible. We started. A nigger, who opened fire on us from about a hundred and fifty yards higher up the mountain, increased our anxiety to gain the fort. Bang! bang! from the head kraal! two bullets just in front of us! Away we went, Hades for leather, hats under our arms, charging through the thorns, dodging in and out in a state of complete funk, until, panting and exhausted, we rolled under the shelter of a friendly schantz. The attack did not last long, no one being hurt on either side, as far as we knew." (P.S. It seems a rather one-sided attack, but Captain Stent mentions "either" side.) "We laughed a good deal over our little escapade when out of danger under the schantz" (and the reader is at liberty to do likewise). Captain Stent proceeds: "Mr. Jenkins is getting better and has asked me to a picnic to-morrow" (I should have stated that Mr. Jenkins, the special *Press* war correspondent, had unfortunately broken his arm). "I have a great respect for '*Jenks*,' but a man who wants to go picnicing up the mountain for amusement! well, what do you think? I have been up the mountain all the week, and to-morrow being Sunday I want to eat my dinner in peace; I want to be sure I shall not be shot at, and that no one will kick my whisky over, while attempting to get out of the way of the big gun's recoil. Also I like a table and a tablecloth, and a proper knife and fork, and smoke and a doss afterwards; and, over and above all, the delightful assurance that no one is taking careful aim at my head from a few yards away. No! I should like to dine with my brother scribblers, but picnics 'is' off."

Sunday, July 29th, on hearing the news of Maláboch's intended surrender, Mr. Jenkins thought it well to celebrate the event by having a picnic up the river. The party consisted of Messrs. Jenkins Ebbage, Amos, Gordon, Stubbs, Fred Neel, Captain

Stent, Dr. Liknaitzky, Waldeck, and myself. How Captain Stent could have imagined there would be any danger, I could not understand. A most delightful spot had been selected close by the water's edge, and the high banks were simply one mass of maidenhair ferns. We were beautifully sheltered by large trees. Jenkins and I had for many days been trying our skill at fishing, but up till then had not even had a solitary bite. We left our rods in the river, secured to the bank some distance from the rendezvous, and then joined our party. Messrs. Amos, Gordon, and Stubbs had been hard at work preparing the luncheon, which was served hot. We were not disturbed at all, and I believe Captain Stent enjoyed his dinner, and had even a tablecloth, a proper knife and fork, also a smoke and a doss afterwards; neither was his whisky kicked over. After spending a most enjoyable afternoon, we returned to look after our fishing-rods, but met with our usual luck, for we caught nothing. While we were here, Neel returned with a rifle and four blank cartridges, accompanied by Townsend, a wounded artilleryman; and as they passed they told us they were going to have some fun with Amos, Stubbs, and Gordon, who were bathing at a forbidden spot. We had not to wait long before we heard two loud reports and a shout from Gordon. "Come along, Dick, the Kafirs are on us!" And Dick (Amos), I was told, with one bound leapt from the water to the top of the opposite bank. Stubbs, who was not quite so good an athlete, took two jumps. During this time Jenkins and I were blowing a whistle and a small tuning trumpet, which resembled in sound the war-horns of the Kafirs, and the fun was kept up for some time, until a laugh from the conspirators relieved the anxiety of the bathers. They then joined us, and we returned to camp in time for the evening service.

Malaboch, as usual, did not keep his word by surrendering, but held out as long as he could.

CHAPTER XXIX.

THE SURRENDER OF MALABOCH.

On Tuesday, 31st July, I made one of another fishing party, the other members being Messrs. Jenkins, Pellat, and Brown; and on our return to the camp after dark, the joyful news awaited us that Malaboch, with his wives and children, had surrendered that afternoon, and was in the Rustenburg fort: not, however, without a desperate but fruitless attempt to break through our wing on the previous night. The first notification of the Chief's intention to give himself up was the receipt by Commandant Malan of a request to be allowed to get some water to wash with, prior to coming out; this was refused, and he was told that if he desired to wash he must go down to the spruit. At about 3.30 in the afternoon, a white flag was seen to emerge from the cave, and a close scrutiny revealed the fact that it was being carried by a small party composed of Malaboch, his two young sons, his brother Papera, four indunas, and about a dozen women. The word was being passed along the lines that Malaboch was coming out, and universal satisfaction was exhibited: men shaking hands with each other, and a general smile being visible on their countenances. Despite the General's orders that all should stand to their posts, there was a general rush to the Rustenburg fort, whither the Chief had wended his way to tender his submission to Commandant Malan. Malaboch looked about thirty years of age, standing five feet ten inches, with somewhat striking features; he wore a slight moustache and beard, and was attired in a light corduroy suit, but had on neither hat nor boots. His two sons, apparently about seven and ten years of age respectively, were also dressed in European costume; the elder of the two was an exceptionally handsome lad. The four indunas were grizzled, determined-looking old veterans, and each wore a metal torque, betokening that he had killed his man. Malaboch wore a most downcast and dejected look, but could not repress an occasional smile at the openly evinced curiosity his appearance excited on all sides. His wives were far superior to those of his women who had previously surrendered, having light skins and good regular features, and took every opportunity of asserting their independence.

Immediately on Malaboch's party arriving at our lines, a strong guard was placed over them, every man holding his gun ready to shoot, in case any attempt to escape should be made. Up to five o'clock only one other native came out from the stronghold, Malaboch stating that as it was so late they would defer their surrender till the morning. On the strength of this information, the order was given to still maintain the cordon of pickets round the Hoofdstad.

About nine o'clock a volley was fired from the direction of Fort Pretoria, which was on the top of the hill about three hundred yards above the stronghold, and it was ascertained that three of the enemy had attempted to break through. In evidence of this a blanket and an assegai were picked up early in the morning. A very strong wind had arisen, accompanied by a dense mist, which completely obscured the krantz on which the Hoofdstad was situated from the view of the vigilant guards. The attempted escape was detected, however, and frustrated by the volley which we heard. Owing to the wretched weather, the pickets spent a most uncomfortable night.

In the course of the evening Malaboch, who was sitting close to a fire, and had but just refused a pinch of snuff, suddenly plunged forward into the fire, falling on his face among the burning embers; he was with difficulty rescued from being burnt to death. Later on, about eleven o'clock, a similar occurrence took place, and he was again badly burnt; his wives now requested the guards to have him tied up, as they insisted that he was trying to commit suicide. On this, Malaboch accused his indunas of being the cause of his leaving the cave, and they in turn retorted that they had repeatedly advised him to pay his taxes, and not make war, but he would not listen to them. The Chief was then made fast in such a manner as to preclude the possibility of his further injuring himself, and at an early hour in the morning Dr. Laxton went over to the fort and dressed his injuries, the chief expressing gratitude for his services.

Soon after daybreak one of the prisoners was sent to the cave with a flag of truce, to try and induce those who were supposed to have remained there to come out without further trouble; he returned with a vague sort of answer, whereupon the signal was given for a general advance upon the Hoofdstad. Daniel Coetzee, Nicholas Vlok, and John Conroy, who had for some weeks been in charge of the friendly natives, proceeded on the right with their forces, whilst Lieutenant Schroeder and the Pretorians took the centre and left positions, being strengthened by Mapen's, Kiviet's and Mathala's Kafirs. Coetzee's contingent was the first to arrive on the spot, and discovered that the cave, or rather the numerous large crevices, were completely deserted, the enemy, who had been holding possession, having disappeared in the most mysterious manner. It was impossible to understand how they broke through our lines, or to form any accurate idea as to where they had gone, unless, indeed, they had betaken themselves to the mountain in the rear. The strange fact of the business was, why, if it was so easy for Malaboch's supporters to effect their escape, the Chief himself did not avail himself of the same opportunity rather than give in, and it is my opinion that the real Malaboch had escaped with his young warriors, especially as none of the latter were captured; it seemed strange that the Chief should surrender himself without his warriors when he had ample means of escaping with them. If our prisoner is Maláboch, then the fact of his surrendering under such circumstances is a puzzle which Maláboch alone can solve.

Twenty-five huts still remained intact, these being hidden amongst the immense boulders. The village itself was enclosed with a strong stockade of thick thornbush and creepers, the approaches consisting of narrow fissures in the rock, protected by schantzes which rendered the position almost impregnable, and had there been any resistance, a large loss of life would of necessity have ensued.

The caves were so situated that it would have been extremely difficult to shoot any of the occupants, and the only means of entrance was by dropping from stone to stone, a distance of from twenty to thirty feet. Very little loot of intrinsic value was found in any of the caves; Conroy and Coetzee succeeded in finding a number of Winchester repeating rifles, and guns of other descriptions, as well as a few karosses, and a very handsome battle-axe, which was believed to have been Maláboch's own; this was presented to Mr. Jenkins, the special correspondent of the *Press*. Considerable dissatisfaction was expressed by these gentlemen at the fact that they were not allowed to retain possession of these guns, inasmuch as it was they who originally scoured the bush, on the condition that they were to keep whatever they looted. The discovery of these Express rifles, together with a case of ammunition, bore out the surmise that certain traders had been reaping a harvest by the sale of the wherewithal for the natives to continue the war.

Amongst other things discovered were Dunsdon's rifle and the cleaning rod of the cannon taken in the affray with the Waterbergers. Two elephants' tusks, weighing between fifty and sixty pounds each, were also taken and eventually sent to the General. Sergeant Lovell Taylor discovered a Kafir pillow with a snuff calabash attached, a battle-axe, and a part of a New Testament, roughly bound at the back with a piece of prepared buckskin. These last findings he presented to me. It was quite possible that other valuables remained in the cave, but a thorough search was a matter of danger and difficulty, owing to the steep sides on which the only foothold obtainable was by means of sticks hammered in at different places, there being several galleries up above, communicating with other chambers; the place occupied by Malaboch and his family being completely screened from danger.

At a quarter past three the General, accompanied by Commandant Trichardt, with an escort, returned to the laager, passing along the line of forts. On arriving at Fort Schroeder, which was within fifty yards of the Hoofdstad, he spoke very kindly to the Pretorians and thanked them for their services; he said he was more than pleased with the way they had conducted themselves during the campaign, and trusted that in every undertaking in life they would be as successful as they had been in their fight against Malaboch. The General paid similar visits to Forts Rensburg, Vorster, and Henning, and ordered the respective garrisons to evacuate them and return to

MEMENTOS FOUND IN HOOFDSTAD.
(*From a photograph by C. H. B. Lovegrove.*)

the laager; an order, needless to say, promptly obeyed.

Yesterday, whilst Maláboch's brother and two other prisoners were being escorted to the Rustenburg laager, one of them attempted to escape, but was recaptured on reaching the bush; he again made a dash for liberty, and was promptly shot through the heart. The Chief's brother was in consequence kept chained.

The joyful news reached us that we were to leave Blaauwberg next morning: many of our Boer friends had already started.

In bidding farewell to the various contingents, the Pretorians carried away with them very pleasant recollections of Laager-Commandant Schutte, who had spared no trouble, in the exercise of his duties, to make camp life pass as pleasantly as possible; had all the Commandants acted in the same manner there would have been far less grumbling and dissension.

CHAPTER XXX.

THE HOSPITAL STAFF—A COUNCIL OF WAR.

The Pretoria relief had arrived and was laagered close to the artillery camp. Their advent was signalled by a series of *feu de joie*, and a number of them proceeded at once to climb the mountain. Orders were heliographed up to Fort Ferreira on Wednesday, August 1st, for all the Pretorians to get ready to come down that afternoon, and prepare for the homeward journey, which would commence the next day.

Sad stories were told by the female prisoners; amongst other things they related how numbers of babies were killed by the shock of exploding shells. In one particular part of the cave, where the women were congregated, it was impossible for them to move without crossing the line of fire. This was on the side nearest the Rustenburg laager, and consequently more than one night was spent by the women lying side by side with the corpses of those killed by the shells, and which they found the greatest difficulty in disposing of.

Dr. Ziervogel arrived on Saturday night (28th July) from Pretoria, with a view to taking charge of the hospital arrangements, but was awaiting comfirmation of his appointment from the General; meanwhile, Dr. Hohls, of Pietersburg, was here, superintending everything in the medical line, Dr. Laxton being on the mountain.

The departure of the Pretoria contingent would be sorely felt in the hospital, for the whole of the medical staff (as already mentioned) had been selected from their numbers, and the greatest praise was due to those who voluntarily elected to undertake the arduous and unpleasant task of attending to the wants of the sick and wounded. They had done such sterling work that it is only right their names should be mentioned; they were Messrs. Idenburg, Van Hoofd, Austin T. Brook, Veyleveldt, R. Hoyle, A. Walters, R. Amos, J. Gordon, and M. Townsend. It would be difficult, indeed, to find men capable of replacing them.

Whilst the Pretorians from Fort Ferreira were returning to laager, I rode with Dr. Liknaitzky to catch a glimpse of the prisoners in the Rustenburg laager, and to bid farewell to the Rev. G. Sonntag. Mr. Sonntag expressed himself with regard to the war in very plain terms. I give his own words: "I am much disgusted with the whole proceedings, and feel very sorry for Malaboch, as I consider he has been most unjustly treated." Bidding the reverend gentleman adieu, we wended our way to the Rustenburg laager, which was close by; there were about a hundred prisoners, mostly very old women and little children. There were a few old men with hoary heads, some of whom appeared to be over a hundred years of age. Malaboch had not come down from the mountain, but was expected in camp that afternoon. We saw his brother, who had tried to escape, with chains fastened to his wrists. On our return to the laager we found that it was broken up, and many of the wagons had already trekked for home. All the members of my mess were busy packing up, and everything was got ready for trekking before we retired.

The next morning, at 10 A.M., a Council of War was held to decide on the disposal of Malaboch. The members consisted of General Joubert, Commandants Erasmus, Malan, Trichardt, Pretorius, Uijs, and Botha, Commissary-General Meyer, and most of the Veld-Cornets. General Joubert, President of the Council, suggested that, before commencing the discussion, those holding only acting right should be sworn in, in order to assure the legal position of the Council, which was done. The President then offered a short prayer, and commenced the proceedings. Commandant Pretorius inquired whether the cattle which he had taken from a friendly chief during his patrol had been returned, as their capture was altogether a mistake. The Commandant then vished to know whether sufficient notice had been given to the natives who had claims, so as to enable them to be present and regain their cattle. Commandant Vorster, of the Commission of War, stated that all the cattle which had been captured in error had been returned to their respective owners. Commandant Pretorius inquired whether the various Commandants,

THE LATE COMMANDANT HENNING PRETORIUS.
(From a photograph by Perrin.)

whose men were engaged in the attack and the retreat, during which the three-pounder was captured by the enemy, and recaptured by our men, had sent in their reports, as they (the reports) would be required by him during the inquiry as to the loss of the gun. He was informed that all reports had been sent in. General Joubert opened the question as to the disposal of the Chief. Commandant Pretorius wished to postpone the discussion until the entire tribe had surrendered, and advised due consideration before the adoption of any harsh measures. General Joubert suggested that Malaboch should be retained as a prisoner of war until the conclusion of the whole campaign, and gave as the reason the opinion that no other Chief would surrender if Malaboch were shot, but would fight to the death. Commandant Pretorius thought that the execution of the Chief would serve as a warning and deterrent to the other Chiefs. The General said it was not part of Kafir nature to profit by example; take, for instance, the hanging of Mampoer.* Commandant Pretorius said that Mampoer was a murderer, as well as a rebel. Then, again, there was the case of Njabel;† but the Commissioner of War pointed out that this Chief surrendered under promise of his life, whereas Malaboch had surrendered unconditionally. Commandant Uijs wished to deal

* Mampoer was hanged in Pretoria for killing a Chief of Sekukuni's country. He was the second captain of Mapoch's country.

† Njabel was fought against for not giving up Mampoer. He was the first captain of Mapoch's country, and is still in Pretoria gaol. The war took place in 1883.

with the case at once. Commandant Erasmus was desirous of instantly making an example of the Chief, and most stringently objected to the case being dealt with by the high court. There appeared to be a general feeling against the high court. One Commandant hoped that the men who had had all the trouble with the Chief would be allowed to try him. The proposal of the President was eventually put, "That Malaboch be retained as a prisoner of war until the termination of the entire campaign." This was passed unanimously. The question of the disposal of the women and children then came up, and after some discussion, it was decided to share them out among the various districts, excepting Waterberg and Zoutpansberg, for five years.

A Kafir god, in the shape of a huge carved crocodile, was brought into camp to-day, amid much beating of drums and blowing of horns. The war-drums, and many of the weapons, were marked with the crocodile. This curiosity is now in the Pretoria Museum.

CHAPTER XXXI.

HOMEWARD BOUND.

ON Thursday, the 2nd August, 1894, we arose at 7 A.M., and had a makeshift breakfast, as nobody felt hungry. We were only too glad to bid farewell to the blue mountains, and about ten we trekked for home. After travelling for nearly two hours we outspanned at a shady place in the veld, and the old style of boiling the kettle while on the route up was resumed. In our eagerness, we set fire, accidentally, to the grass round about, which spread rapidly, but was extinguished before damage was done. We spanned in again at 3 P.M.; the roads were so bad that we all had to get down and push, the wheels being deeply embedded in the sand. The next morning, desiring to reach home as soon as possible, we trekked at two o'clock, and outspanned at six, near a kraal. We were very short of oxen, only ten in each wagon, and those very poor. Nothing more important than the ordinary vexations of travel on South African roads occurred till we arrived at Tibaan's Loop, where so much bartering took place on our journey up. We visited the various kraals, where there was a great beer drink on. Numbers of young girls were marching round the huts singing.

The married and elder women were more or less drunk, and, for our amusement, engaged in hand-to-hand conflicts, with dried amabele stalks for weapons, slashing each other savagely over the bare shoulders, and raising huge weals.

I asked to see the Chief, and was directed to his hut. On calling to him, he crawled out on his hands and knees; he, too, had been imbibing too freely, but had sense enough to understand that I was a Mfundisi, and was desirous of speaking to his people. He was somewhat grumpy at my request, but yielded, and gathered together about thirty, who sat down in a semicircle, he in their midst. As they had all been drinking very heavily, I spoke to them of the evils of intemperance. This was too much for the Chief, who evidently felt very uncomfortable. He got up, and went away, excusing himself by saying that he was very old, and could not sit in that position for long at a time. Messrs. Eddie Cooper and Fred McArthur acted as interpreters. The Chief informed me that the young girls present were still at school, and that he had invited them to his feast, which would last three months. We trekked on about four, and outspanned three hours afterwards close to the Chief Mathala's house. Next day, Sunday, we trekked on as far as the mission station, and I called, with Lieutenant Holzer, on our friend, the Rev. Mr. Parisius. He seemed much depressed, and Mrs. Parisius was ill. I soon learned the reason for this depression and illness. On our journey up, I observed a fine little fellow, two and a half years of age, whom I now missed. I asked where he was, and with much emotion Mr. Parisius informed me that his bright little son had expired of croup four weeks ago. I held service in the camp at 10.30, at which Mr. Parisius was present. After the service, he very kindly presented us with a number of oranges, and these were much enjoyed, as the day was very hot. I then, with Mr. Tischer (a German), attended the native service in the mission chapel. It was very impressive, and Mr. Parisius, who is gifted with a rich voice, led the singing. We joined them at dinner, and soon after, Lieutenant Holzer came. Mrs. Parisius looked very ill. Their little daughter, aged about nine, was exceptionally quiet, and seemed to feel the loss of the companionship of her little brother very keenly. Mr. Parisius took us into his garden, where we gathered more oranges from the trees. The kindness and hospitality of this gentleman I much appreciated. He rejoiced with us at the success of the campaign, and wished us Godspeed. We thanked our kind host and hostess, and bade them adieu.

During the next trek Gerard and G. Waldeck took their guns and left the wagons on a search for game. They brought back a few partridges and pheasants, which agreeably varied our fare. There was very little sport to be had, as the veld was ablaze—this being the grass burning season. Our next outspan was at Biltongfontein. One wagon, occupied exclusively by Hollanders, broke down during this trek, but was fixed up for the time being. Here (at

Biltongfontein) we had some shooting practice, and Gerard proved to be the best shot, bringing the objects shot at down twice in succession. I accompanied Gerard, Waldeck, and Austin Brook on a koodoo hunt, but without result, our only bag being a plump partridge. Returning to the wagons we found that the game shot by Waldeck and Gerard had already been cooked, and we had a most sumptuous repast. Our bill of fare was as follows: roast pheasant, roast partridge, jugged hare, potatoes, preserved cabbage (this latter being part of the dainties provided by Mrs. Henshall on our leaving Pretoria), blanc-mange, rusks, cocoa, and coffee. The next morning we were off again at five and reached Pietpotgietersrust at 7.15. I visited the village school, kept by Mr. Botha; I was accompanied by Gerard, Lovell Taylor, Mauritz Preller, Jacques du Troit, J. Nel, and A. Walters. Mr. Botha, uncle to Gerard, invited me to examine the children, which I did; they were well advanced in grammar, geography, reading, writing, and arithmetic.

Their singing was really good, and reflected great credit on the schoolmaster and his able assistant, Miss Pretorius. We stayed for two hours, much to the delight of Mr. Botha, and our visit certainly gave pleasure to the youngsters, especially when I recommended a half holiday, which was granted. After calling on Mrs. Ross, to whom I was introduced by R. Amos, we continued our journey. We met the Rev. Mr. Faure, the Dutch minister, who was returning in his buggy from Waterberg, after having held a service there. The reverend gentleman exchanged friendly greeting with us, and each party went on its way.

At our next outspan I sent a telegram to the Bishop, informing him that we hoped to reach Pretoria on the 14th or 15th August.

About one hundred wagons passed us here and nearly four hundred men, who were on their way to the low country, and were to relieve the Rustenburgers. Lovell Taylor offered a bandolier to one of the Boers for seven shillings and sixpence. He took it away to his wagon and straightway disappeared in the dust raised by the train of wagons— there was nothing more seen of the Boer or the bandolier, which belonged, not to Lovell Taylor (he was commissioned only to sell it), but to Gerard, and was his own private property and not part of the Goverment equipment. We soon reached Buiskop in the Waterberg District, and only a few miles from the warm baths. The trees just here were simply one mass of white blossom, resembling the English May, and were, indeed, a striking sight.

Lieutenant Holzer, Acting Veld-Cornet, left for Nylstroom to buy trek cattle, as we had great difficulty in proceeding with the animals that had been with us at the front. He secured twenty, with which we made reasonable progress.

On Saturday, August 11th, we arrived at the Warm Baths Hotel. We were all very glad to reach this delightful spot once more, and to meet the genial host and hostess, Mr. and Mrs. Kaiser, who spared no pains in making everybody as comfortable as possible. In the evening, through the forethought and exertions of Messrs. Vogts and J. Tischer, a concert was held in the dining-room. The proceedings were much enhanced by the presence of visitors from Pretoria. They were, Mr. and Mrs. J. D. Celliers, Mr. and Mrs. Maughan, Mr. and Mrs. Neal, and Mrs. Visser. The programme was as follows:—

PIANO SOLO	. . . .	Mr. de Voogd.
SONG	"Malaboch."	Mr. Kenny Shepherd.
SONG	"The Scout."	Mr. Neal.
SONG	"The Vagabond."	Mr. Austin Brook.
SONG	"The Maid of the Mill."	Mr. R. Hoyle.
SONG	"The Powder Monkey."	Mr. Claridge.
PIANO SOLO	. . . .	Mr. Kaiser.
SONG	"Comrades."	Mr. T. Anderson.
SONG	"For Me."	Mrs. Visser.
SONG	"The Old Horse."	Mr. Maughan.
SONG	"Schwiegerman."	Mr. K. Schmidt.
SONG	"Nancy Lee."	Mr. Chas. Lever.
SONG	"The Midshipmite."	Rev. Colin Rae.
SONG	"Ting-a-Ling."	Mr. A. Walters.
SONG	"Rameaux."	Mr. de Voogd.
RECITATION	. . . .	Mr. J. D. Celliers.
DUET	"Larboard Watch."	Mr. Austin Brook & Rev. Colin Rae.
SONG (by special request)	"Malaboch."	Dr. Tobias (the composer).
SONG	"Mary and John."	Mr. A. Walters.

Mr. J. D. Celliers occupied the chair, with Lieutenant Holzer in the vice-chair. Messrs. de Voogd and D. Kaiser were the accompanists. The great catch of the evening was, of course, the song "Malaboch," which was rendered in grand style by Dr. Tobias.

The next morning (Sunday, August 12th), through the kindness of Mr. Kaiser, I held a religious service in the drawing-room of the hotel. Mr. Kaiser was good enough to accompany the hymns on his piano. It had been arranged that the whole of the contingent should dine at the hotel, but owing to one of our men attacking and half killing the coolie cook, this idea had to be abandoned, much to the disgust of all, as our provisions were very scarce. The wagons started at 3 o'clock. Lieutenant Schroeder invited me to stay with him at the hotel as his guest, intending to catch up the wagons at the Thorns. Mr. J. Conroy was good enough to leave his horse behind for my use. In the evening we held a sacred concert, and retired at 10.30.

Soon after I had entered my room, I noticed a black uneven streak on the pillow-case. Thinking it to be a piece of string, I attempted to remove it, when lo and behold! to my horror, it was full of life; the supposed string was nothing but large red ants. I knocked up Schroeder, who was next door, and on our searching further, we came across thousands of these horrid creatures racing over the quilt; some of them started flying. In one part of the room there was a mass of these insects—simply a lump of legs, wings, and bodies of ants, some six inches by three, and quivering with life; I never saw such a thing before nor since. Mr. Kaiser came in with some Keating's powder, and as he sprinkled it freely about the bed, remarked: "This will soon make them trek." However, they didn't trek quick enough for me to occupy that room, and I wish here to express my obligations to Lieutenant Schroeder, who most courteously gave up his room for my use; thus adding one more to the many acts of kindness and consideration for which I am indebted to this gentleman.

The following day, in company of Mesdames Visser and Maughan and Mr. Doré, we enjoyed some good croquet. Mr. Doré, who was an invalid, had come here to benefit his health, by bathing in the warm springs which burst from the ground, and from which the place derives its name. In the afternoon the ladies, Lieutenant Schroeder, and myself were driven to Potgieter's farm. We were most courteously received by Mr., Mrs., and Miss Potgieter. A feature of the farm was a fruit garden, wherein all kinds of tropical fruit-trees thrived, more especially the orange and banana. On the orange-trees were fruit and blossom at the same time—quite a novelty to me. Mr. Potgieter kindly invited us to take away as much of the ripe fruit as we could carry—an invitation which we heartily availed ourselves of, and we then returned to the hotel. Mr. Kaiser gave us a most pressing invitation to stay the night as his guests; but this we could not do, as it would take us all our time to catch up with the train of wagons before they reached the Thorns.

At 10.30 P.M., we (Lieutenant Schroeder and myself) started off on our ride, by the light of the moon. R. Amos, who had also been the guest of Lieutenant Schroeder, undertook to act as our guide, saying that he knew the road well. We therefore followed his lead, which resulted first in our rousing a white man at a wayside house to inquire the way. He told us to retrace our steps some three hours; in attempting to do this we got more lost than we were before, and roused some Kafirs in a kraal; then some "*boys*" sleeping in a scotch cart, and by their united directions, about three in the morning, came to a signboard on the roadside marked (in English), "to the warm baths," which was very disappointing. Day was now breaking and we could form some idea of the way we should *not* take; so by the process of exhaustion, we started off again, this time in the right road, and arrived about 4.30 at Valboschfontein. Here we offsaddled, fed our horses, and slept for two hours, reaching Pienaars River, in the wake of the wagons, in time for breakfast. We met a young fellow named Bowmaker, who was *en route* from Pretoria to Pietersburg, on a bicycle. Pienaars River is some forty miles from Pretoria, and Bowmaker was five and a half hours out. Schroeder's horse had gone lame before we reached this place, and in consequence we stayed longer than we had intended; it was half-past eleven before we were in the saddle again. The horse's lameness got worse as we proceeded, and we had to leave the animal at Haman's kraal, Schroeder procuring another mount there. Then we rode on to Lewis's Store, reaching there about 1.30 P.M., thence to Waterval at 6 P.M., where we caught up to the wagons, and dined; later on riding forward to the Thorns (the scene of the potclay incident on the way up), where we camped for the night. At five the following morning, Lieutenant Schroeder roused me and we rode on, in advance of the wagons to Wonderboom, reaching there at 6.30 in the morning. At this place we waited for the Reception Committee. Dr. Mader, Messrs. Reno, Gates, Barrett, and Eddie Cooper (the latter having ridden into Pretoria the previous night) were among the first to arrive. We filled up the time with rifle practice and football.

CHAPTER XXXII

TRIUMPHAL ENTRY INTO PRETORIA—THE RECEPTION COMMITTEE—THE PRESIDENT'S SPEECH.

The following is taken in great part from the *Press* of the 18th August, 1894 :—

We arrived at Wonderboom Poort on Wednesday morning, the 15th August, just twelve weeks from the date of our departure. We were not there long before the town civilian contingent met us. Every horse and every vehicle in the place must have been brought into requisition, and the road to Wonderboom Poort was thronged with a succession of vehicles, cyclists, horsemen, and pedestrians.

The road is, in all conscience, dusty enough on ordinary occasions, but in this particular instance it surpassed itself. With a cross wind blowing, the sand simply flew into one's eyes, ears, and mouth, as it was ploughed up by the various methods of progression adopted.

We were all in the best of health, some being bronzed and bearded almost beyond recognition, in consequence of exposure to sun and air, and non-exposure to the barber.

As carriage after carriage drove up we were met by friends, and heartily congratulated on our safe return.

The original arrangement was to start from Wonderboom at 2.30, so that the triumphal entry into Pretoria might be made about 3.30, but (strange for South Africa) everything got a little ahead of its appointed time. The cabs chartered to convey us turned up about the time they (the cabs) should have left Church Square; and as there was an evident anxiety to start, the Cab Committee set to work. There was little difficulty in this operation, for the men were quite as eager to get to sweethearts and wives, as sweethearts and wives were to receive them. A green sash, on which was sewn a vierkleur rosette, was distributed to every member of the returning troops, and then a start was made at about two o'clock. Veld-Cornet Melt Marais had previously arrived in charge of the Volunteer Cavalry, and as the cavalcade was being got in order, he renewed acquaintance with old friends of the contingent. He also brought a letter for me from the Bishop, welcoming us back and inviting me to stay at *Bishop's Cote*. If ever a man deserved to have his arm ache for a week from hearty hand-shaking, Melt Marais was that man.

After Mr. Haarhoff had succeeded in getting the vehicles in something like order, the carriages containing the members of the Executive and sub-Committees led the way, the cavalry acting as advance guard.

The first carriage contained Mr. J. S. Smit, Chairman of the Committee, and Mr. Loots, Secretary; next came a landau carrying Mr. James, Lieutenant Holzer, Mr. Buykes, and Dr. Lenshoek; then followed another four-wheeler with Mr. Jahn, Acting Veld-Cornet Charles Rice, and Mr. Vivian Otto. There were several other carriages containing members of the Committee and sub-Committees, whose names are mentioned further on.

Behind the Committee came the cabs containing the unmounted men of the contingent. It was noticeable that the horses did not appear to have stood the campaign as well as the men, for most of them were rather low in condition, showing more ribs than flesh. When passing the Pelican Club Mr. Parker came out and waved the National flag, and was heartily cheered.

Nearing Mr. Eloff's house, the length of the procession could be judged. Including the private vehicles which fell in the rear, there must have been a string over a mile in length. There was a large concourse of people at Arcadia Bridge; the Infantry Volunteers had been drawn up there with the band, under Bandmaster Amorisson (who, by the way, had licked his men into decent shape in a very short time). Mr. Eddie Meintjes was also in evidence with the red, white, blue, and green. Here a halt was called; the band formed up, and the volunteers shouldered their rifles, and the march continued through Church Street East to Church Square. It was an inspiriting spectacle. The side walks were crowded with onlookers from the bridge to the square; every popular demonstration that tact, thought, and affection could supply was given, including loud cheers and waving of handkerchiefs. We were utterly astounded at the enthusiasm displayed in welcoming us, and thoroughly appreciated the great kindness and self-denying efforts of our warm-hearted Pretoria friends.

Banners and mottoes met our eyes at every turn; even the blue gum-trees in the Arcadia Avenue had been made use of to display the Transvaal flag. Nothing prettier in the way of decorations had ever been seen in Pretoria, and we were bid " Welcome," in English and Dutch, from many a house-front. The following gentlemen constituted the various Committees :—Concert : Messrs. Serrurier, Cronin, E. P. A. Meintjes, Petrie, and Tuke. Cabs : Messrs. A. C. Meintjes, Cronin, and H. F. Strange. Sashes : Messrs. Botha, Vorstman, Buykes, and Percy Levy. Decorations : Messrs. Serrurier, Leo. Weinthal, Van Vouw, De Wildt, and Bouchamp. Executive : Messrs. Wolff, Vorstman, Dr. Engelenburg, Haarhoff, and Dr. Knobel.

Later on the men were addressed at the Landdrost's office by Landdrost Schutte and Commissioner Smit; the latter, in very complimentary terms, referring to the military discipline and soldierly conduct of the Pretoria contingent. Mr. E. P. A. Meintjes then read the address of welcome; an engraving from a photograph by Mr. C. H. B. Lovegrove, of Lydenburg, is given on the opposite page.

A copy of the address, which was designed and lithographed at the Pretoria *Press* works, was presented by the proprietors to each of the members of the contingent. An adjournment was then made to the Government buildings, where His Honour the

ADDRESS OF WELCOME.

State President addressed the commando. His Honour, standing up in his carriage, said :—

"Burghers, Friends, and New-Comers,—I have much pleasure in welcoming back the men who willingly went to the front. It is a source of pleasure for me to state—it has, indeed, given me much gratification—that I have never heard of a single complaint or of a single act of disobedience on the part of those who were commandeered, neither from the burghers nor from the aliens. On the contrary, you have willingly gone, and willingly entered into the rocks, into the dark caves, and brought forth the enemy. I have not heard of any disobedience, but obediently have you proceeded on your mission, and you have hauled out the enemy. Aye, even so brave were you that you would not stop at the foot of the mountain, but insisted to storm the same, in order to drive the enemy from his stronghold in the caves. By doing this you have given me proof of your faithfulness to the South African Republic, the State you have accepted as your fatherland. I do not desire to make a distinction between nationalities, as far as the franchise is concerned, but only between those who are faithful, and you, most of you, who are strangers, have now shown, in connection with this war, that you sympathise with us. For this reason it is my intention, without the necessity for any alteration in the franchise law, to frame a list on which the names of those men who have so willingly fought in the country's cause shall appear, and submit the same to the Volksraad. They have, gentlemen, identified themselves, as far as fealty and fidelity to the State are concerned, with the old burghers. And not only to you whom I now address does this apply, but it extends to all the men of all the districts who have gone willingly to the call of duty, and who are now absent and cannot hear what I say this day; but I doubt not there is someone present who will record the words I speak. In times of peace a man has many friends, but in the hour of danger one learns who are his real friends. Again I thank you for your loyalty, and wish you, with all my heart, welcome home. And before I close, one single word to my friends in the town; some of our men have not yet arrived. They are coming in charge of the enemy. Give them also an honourable reception; they also deserve it well. I have said."

His Honour then left his carriage and disappeared within the precincts of the Government buildings, and an adjournment was then made to the old Standard Bank, where refreshments were partaken of. There Mr. Serrurier eulogised Colonel Ferreira and Lieutenant Charles Rice, toasting them with musical honours. The assembly was also addressed by Messrs. Meintjes, J. W. Leonard, Dr. Leyds, State Secretary, and Mr. Ewald Esselen, State Attorney. Commissioner Smit, Mr. Zeiler, and others entered the room and fraternised with the men, shaking hands all round. At the request of Mr. Esselen and Dr. Leyds, the Commando Choir sang the song "Malaboch," and the proceedings shortly after terminated.

I then availed myself of the Bishop's kind invitation by proceeding to *Bishop's Cote*. After dinner his Lordship and Mrs. Bousfield accompanied me to Burger's Park, where a promenade concert was given in honour of the returned warriors; the music was discoursed by the volunteer band, but we only stayed a short time, and I retired early, having spent a pleasant, though very tiring and trying day.

[*To face page* 204.

HIS HONOUR S. J. P. KRUGER,
STATE PRESIDENT, Z.A.R.

CHAPTER XXXIII.

THE ARRIVAL OF MALABOCH IN PRETORIA—DEATH OF DR. TOBIAS—ST. AUGUSTINE'S BROTHERHOOD—I GO TO ROODEPOORT, AND FROM THENCE TO PILGRIM'S REST.

THE next day the Rustenburgers arrived at Wonderboom with their prisoner and his followers, and there awaited instructions. I was driven out from Pretoria with Canon Fisher and Lieutenant Holzer, and, on our arrival, we saw a number of natives (I think about one hundred and fifty men) squatting on the ground, but the absence of young men was very noticeable. Maláboch and his indunas were secured in a wagon. I climbed on to the Voorkist and asked him if he were really Maláboch, and where all his fighting men were, as nearly all our prisoners were decrepit old men. Whereupon he said that his nephew was with the prisoners and would tell me all about it, as he could speak English well. I soon found his nephew, who assured me that the prisoner in the wagon was his Uncle Maláboch, and the young men were those I saw around me. This last piece of information was simply prevaricating. I think there can be no doubt that the young men had made good their escape. The Chief's lips still bore signs of his recent burns caused by falling in the fire on the top of the mountain, just after his surrender.

We returned in time to see them brought in. The burghers rode to the Raadzaal, where the President awaited them, and, standing on the steps, His Honour asked the Commandant whether the prisoner he had brought in was the rebel Chief Malaboch, and being satisfied with his reply, congratulated the burghers on their success, and then ordered the removal of the prisoners to the State gaol, where the Chief still remains.

I remained the guest of the Bishop and Mrs. Bousfield until the 22nd August, Mrs. Bousfield, with great consideration, allowing me to make my own arrangements for spending my time. The week, which would have been one of the pleasantest I have spent in South Africa, was saddened by the deaths of the Rev. Father Douglas, Dr. F. B. Tobias, and Mr. John Meyer.

The Bishop left to-day (August 16th) on a visit to Boksburg. The time between this and Sunday passed very rapidly.

As the late warriors promenaded the streets, quite a metamorphosis was observed in their general appearance; razors had been used and store-clothes donned. The change is well represented in the accompanying engraving, from a photograph by Mr. Reginald Shepherd, of Pretoria, where two of my comrades-in-arms are shown in their war-paint, the others being in the garb of town-life.

[*To face page* 206.

MR. EWALD ESSELEN (LATE STATE ATTORNEY).

On Sunday morning, the 19th August, while on my way to the Cathedral, I was informed for the first time of the death of Dr. F. B. Tobias by Mr. Meynhardt, one of the late doctor's messmates.

I was shocked and unnerved at this sad news. It appeared that the night previous, Dr. Tobias, while dining with his bosom friend, Dr. Mader, complained of insomnia. Morphia was hypodermically injected before he retired, and on his boy entering the room with coffee the next morning, he found the doctor to be dead, with his faithful dog alongside him on the bed.

The cause of death was conjestion of the brain. On the news becoming known, the town was thrown into profound grief, great sorrow being expressed by his friends, especially those of the legal profession.

The funeral took place the next day at 3.30 P.M., and was attended by his late comrades, under command of Lieutenant Schroeder.

All the men wore their campaign uniform, and marched to the residence of the deceased, and from thence to the cemetery. His former messmates bore the coffin from the entrance of the cemetery to the grave. Members of the bar and side-bar were present in large numbers, as were also Dr. Leyds, State Secretary, Mr. Ewald Esselen, State Attorney, Chief Justice Kotzé, Judges Jorrisen, Korte, and Morice, Advocates Leonard, Cloete, Coster, and Kleyn.

Addresses were delivered at the graveside by the Rev. Van Belkum, of the Dutch Reformed Church, and myself.

The deceased was forty-three years of age, and was born at Probolengo, East Indies.

On my return from the cemetery, Mr. Sam Jones, of the Union Club, informed me of the death of Mr. John Meyer, of the *Press* Editorial Staff, from whom I had parted only two days before, he being then apparently in good health. Mr. Jones had been most assiduous in attending to the wants of the dying man, and at the doctor's suggestion, Mr. Meyer was removed from the Union Club to the Pretoria Hospital, only two hours before his death. In spite of appearances to the contrary, Mr. Meyer had enjoyed but indifferent health for some time past.

He was born at Woodstock, near Cape Town, and was only thirty-seven years of age. The funeral took place in Pretoria on Tuesday, the 21st August, the service of the English Church being conducted by the Rev. J. W. Llewelyn and myself.

Returning to *Bishop's Cote*, I heard from Mrs. Bousfield of the death of the Rev. Father Douglas, the Superior of St. Augustine's Brotherhood at Modderpoort, in the Orange Free State. I have most pleasant recollections of this community, having stayed there for a few days while on my way to Basutoland in 1890; and, on my return to the diamond fields early the following year, I spent a very happy month there. I can never forget the kind Father, whose health, even then, was failing him. His happy face, cheery voice, and kindly disposition endeared him to all with whom he came into contact. To know him was to love him. He

DR. W. J. LEYDS,
LATE STATE SECRETARY OF THE SOUTH AFRICAN REPUBLIC.

was universally popular, not only in his immediate surroundings, but throughout the whole of South Africa. The great secret of this lay in his utterly unselfish nature and thorough spirituality; he had but one motive in life, and that was to bring souls to the knowledge of God. His keen perception and tact, in conjunction with a beautiful sympathy in dealing with the souls of men, well fitted him for his high calling.

The influence of such a devoted life of self-sacrifice has been, and is still, widely felt. Well may it be said of this departed servant of God—"He being dead, yet speaketh."

Through the courtesy of the Rev. Father Carmichael I am able to give the following interesting account of St. Augustine's:—

The inception of St. Augustine's Brotherhood was due to the first Bishop of Bloemfontein (Dr. Twells), who, from his admiration of what he saw of collegiate and religious life at Cambridge, and from reading, formed ideas as to a missionary Brotherhood for his diocese. In 1865, he wrote a letter of extraordinary power to his friends in England suggesting such a thing. In 1866, Canon Beckett, of Cumbrae, and Curate of Elford, was found to head the movement.

He published a letter appealing for men and means early in 1867, and went to Oxford and elsewhere, and obtained men, and promises from more to follow. He sailed on Ascension Day, 1867; met Bishop Twells at Algoa Bay, July 13th, on his way home to the Pan-Anglican Conference.

The Brotherhood travelled by wagon from Port

Elizabeth to Bloemfontein, where Dean Croghan met them. The Bishop, in 1866, bought two farms in the conquered territory for his "Brotherhood," and had laid a foundation-stone there February 2nd, 1867. The war with the Basutos breaking out a second time, prevented the Brotherhood from occupying them at once; so they settled for nearly a year at Springfield, a farm eight miles from Bloemfontein, and on the road to Thaba Nchu. Thence they moved to Thaba Nchu in 1868, and, while there, built a church and mission-house. One of the Brotherhood party (Terry) was a builder. In April, 1869, they reached Modderpoort, where they first lived in a cave and huts built about it. Services and school were held in the cave.

In 1868, Bishop Twells again left England, and brought a few more recruits for the party (one was Canon Doxat, now in the Corea). In 1869, some more recruits came, headed by Canon Bevan, and they began a Dutch, Sesuto, and European work, which has gone on ever since. The church was built and consecrated on St. Paul's Day, 1872.

A house and beautiful gardens were laid out and a native school built. All this was at Modderpoort. Through the Brotherhood, churches were also built at Ladybrand, six miles from Modderpoort; at Ficksburg, thirty miles away; and at Clocolan, a distance of eighteen miles.

A native school and work were also established in Ladybrand. Many of the early members of the Brotherhood undertook works in other parts of the

[*To face page* 210.

THE STATE PRISONER, MALABOCH, IN THE PRETORIA GAOL.

diocese, the Diamond Fields, Phillipolis, Fauresmith, and Thaba Nchu; others are now working in other dioceses in South Africa. The longest to remain of the original number at Modderpcort was Brother John (Rev. J. E. Williams), who, being one of the original party, remained till 1879. The Rev. Father Douglas was asked by Bishop Webb in 1878 to relieve Canon Beckett, whose age was then fifty-nine. This he did, and reached Modderpoort in April, 1879. He at once threw himself into all Canon Beckett's itinerating work, and drew more members to the community, and put it more definitely on the basis of the "Religious Life." When he died, August 19th, 1894, full of labours, and having drawn the affections of the whole neighbourhood, he left the Brotherhood and its works in a way in which it could continue to develop. Father Sanderson was elected Superior in his place, and it now numbers two priest brethren and two lay brethren. But though few out of the many who have stayed and lived in the Brotherhood home have found their vocation in it, many have found a vocation through it, and are doing good works in South Africa or elsewhere, and so have profited by its existence.

Canon Beckett died February 22nd, 1885, and is buried at Modderpoort.

Father Douglas was best known in England, before he came to South Africa, as a great mission preacher and ardent lover of souls and worker for them. He was Canon Body's curate at Kirby Misperton, and then (1875-8) a member of the Stoke-upon-Terne Brotherhood in the Lichfield diocese.

By the afore-mentioned deaths of three of my friends, the kind Bishop's desire to give me a week's pleasure and relaxation before undertaking my duties at Roodepoort was sadly frustrated.

I left Pretoria on Wednesday the 22nd August, as the Bishop had arranged for me to meet him at Johannesburg Station that day.

Arriving there, I found his Lordship awaiting me, and we then proceeded by the same train to Roodepoort.

While on our way from the Roodepoort Station to call on Mr. George Alfred Goodwin, manager of the United Main Reef Gold Mining Company, the Bishop suddenly stood still, and, raising his hat, an example which I followed, offered a short prayer that the work there might be accepted and blessed.

On reaching Mr. Goodwin's house we were kindly received and entertained by the late Mrs. Goodwin. We then visited the Assembly Hall, where the services were held (lent for this purpose by the trustees); and after calling on Mrs. Saunderson, who provided us with luncheon, we retraced our steps to the railway station. I had some difficulty in finding suitable apartments, and this much concerned the Bishop. Eventually, through the kindness of Mr. Goodwin, I was accommodated with a room at the Company's staff quarters.

My stay in Roodepoort was but for a few months; during that short time, however, I made many friends, amongst whom I wish to especially mention Mr. and Mrs. Goodwin, Mr. and Mrs. Skinner, Messrs. F.

[*To face page* 212.

LOVEDAY. FRED NEEL.
JENKINS. REV. C. RAE. R. AMOS.
R. SHEPHERD. EBBAGE.

METAMORPHOSED WARRIORS.

Runchman and A. Alston (with whom I lived), Malcolmson, Buckland, M. Wilson, G. Bottomley and G. Mason (the two latter, I regret to say, are since deceased), Miss Mason (now Mrs. Adcock), Messrs. Nethersole, Parker, Balfour, and Bradley, Mr. and Mrs. George North (Mrs. North with her two children were killed in the railway accident mentioned in the Appendix), the Misses Rorke (now Mrs. Balfour and Mrs. Bradley), Mr. and Mrs. Penny, Mr., Mrs., and Miss Noble, Mr. W. Dixon, Mrs. Peacock, Misses McMaster, Mr. and Mrs. Atherstone, and Miss Couper.

My sphere of work included the suburb of Maraisburg, about four miles from Roodepoort, where I held service on Sunday morning, as well as devoting one day every week to visiting. I was encouraged in my work here by the kindness of the people generally, and was much interested in the work of the school, conducted by Miss Gertie Smith and her able assistant Miss Lizzie Malan.

The following much appreciated my work amongst them, and did all in their power to help it forward: Dr. W. P. Johnstone, Mr. and Mrs. Hellman, Mr. and Mrs. Steele, Mr. and Mrs. Malan and family, Mr. and Mrs. McKechnie, Mr. and Mrs. F. Smith, Mr. and Mrs. W. Smith, Mr. and Mrs. Secretan, Miss Gertie Smith, Miss Lizzie Malan (who acted as organist and performed her honorary duties most faithfully), Miss Ilva Frames (now Mrs. Steil), and Mr. Hall.

During my stay here I received the following

flattering letter from Mr. Attorney Rice (late Acting Veld-Cornet during the Malaboch campaign) :—

PRETORIA, 14th September, 1894.

DEAR MR. RAE,—Could you make it convenient to run over to Pretoria some day next week to give us an opportunity of presenting you with a souvenir and a purse, subscribed for by numerous friends, admirers, and comrades, as a slight recognition of your services during the Malaboch campaign.

Kindly let me know by return post. Yours truly,
C. G. RICE.

This presentation was made in the presence of many of my old comrades by Dr. Leyds, State Secretary, at the Transvaal Hotel, and consisted of a gold hunter watch, with monogram engraved on the cover and an inscription inside, and a purse of sovereigns. This evidence of good-fellowship is greatly prized by me.

Mr. Ewald Esselen, State Attorney, who was unable to be present, excused his absence in a letter to Mr. Rice.

After leaving Roodepoort I was the guest of Dr. Johnstone, Mrs. Johnstone being in England at the time. From there I came to Pilgrim's Rest, in the district of Lydenburg.

COMRADES OF THE LATE DR. TOBIAS.
Just before the Funeral.

[*To face page* 214.

GLOSSARY.

Aapies	Monkeys.
Amabele	Kafir corn; millet.
Beeker	Tin pannikin (about ¾ lb. measure).
Berg	Mountain.
Blaauwberg	Blue mountain.
Boer meal	Cornflour not dressed.
Boy	Native men in South Africa are usually designated "boys."
Brackish	Saltish.
Bucksail	Tarpaulin.
Burghers	Strictly speaking, men on active service, but now generally applied to enfranchised citizens.
Calabash	Drinking vessel made from a pumpkin.
Commandeered	The law of conscription in the Transvaal. British subjects and civil servants are personally exempt, but not their goods.
Doppers	Members of a religious sect, the Ana-Baptists. The word "dopper" is probably derived from the old Dutch "dorper," a name contemptuously applied during the Middle Ages to residents in Dutch towns.
Drift	Ford.
Euphorbia	A poisonous plant abounding in acrid milk.
Guerilla	Irregular; troops not disciplined.
Hoofdstad	Literally, "chief city." Generally applied to residences or capitals of native chiefs.
Insangu	Wild hemp; smoked by the natives as a narcotic.

Kloof	Cleft, chasm, ravine.
Knobneusen	Literally, "swollen noses." The appellation of a native tribe in Zoutpansberg.
Kopje	Mound, hillock.
Kraal	Literally, sheep or cattle-pen; also a term generally applied to native villages in South Africa.
Krantz	Precipice.
Krijsraad	Council of War.
Land en Volk	Land and people.
Landdrost	Magistrate.
Loot	Literally, "lottery"; cattle, etc., taken in war; the spoil.
Mfundisi	Clergyman.
Muid	(Dutch "mud"); a bag holding about 200 lbs. of grain.
Mealies	Indian corn; maize.
Nek	Mountain pass.
Nijlstroom	Literally, "Nile Stream." The name of a village and river in Waterberg. "Nijl" signifies Nile, and "stroom" stream.
Predikant	Clergyman or preacher.
Raadzaal	Literally, "council chamber"; applied to the legislative halls.
Salamander	Horney-backed lizard.
Scherm	Screen or fence made of bush interwoven. The word is also applied to anything constructed as a protection against wind or rain.
Span	Team.
Spruit	Rivulet.
Tickey	Threepenny-piece.
Trek	To pull.
Uitlander	Outlander; a foreigner.
Utyala	Kafir beer made from amabele.
Veld-Cornet	A Government official who has charge of a ward, and, in time of war, ranks as captain.
Vierkleur	Literally, the "four colours"; applied to the Transvaal flag.

[*To face page* 216.

THE LATE REV. FATHER DOUGLAS, S.S.J.

Volkslied	. .	The Transvaal National Anthem.
Volksraad	. .	Literally, the "People's Council," the Parliament of the Transvaal.
Voorkist	. .	Literally, "front box." Boer wagons generally have boxes in front which serve as repositories for odds and ends and seats for drivers.
Voorlooper	. .	Literally, "front walker"; applied to boys who lead bullock teams.

ST. AUGUSTINE'S BROTHERHOOD, MODDERPOORT, LADYBRAND, O.F.S.

[*To face page* 218.

APPENDIX.

THE JOHANNESBURG CRISIS.

THE first news of this now historical event reached Pilgrim's Rest, a busy little gold-mining camp situated near the eastern boundary of the Transvaal and about two hundred miles from Pretoria, on the evening of the 31st December, 1895. Startling rumours soon spread through the camp to the effect that Dr. Jameson, Administrator of Rhodesia, with eight hundred of the Charterland troops, fully armed with Maxims, field pieces, and Lee-Metford rifles, had actually crossed the western border of the Transvaal, and were to meet the burghers, two thousand strong, in an open encounter near Krugersdorp at ten the next morning. The telegraph office was kept open all night in consequence. Suppressed excitement prevailed, and Mr. Willis, telegraphist in temporary charge, was kept busy, but with Government messages only, the use of the wire being debarred from the general public. The night was pitch dark, and I was sitting in my room working at my manuscript, assisted by Mr. Dan Matthews. Whilst we were thus engaged, our attention was suddenly drawn to the blowing of a bugle. The various calls were blown in such a manner that we concluded the blower was no expert in that line. At first we thought that a "krijsraad" was being summoned by the Mining Commissioner, Mr. J. S. Joubert, but after we had heard the "Volkslied" followed immediately by "God save the Queen," our minds were set at rest, and we once more resumed our work. We adjourned to the church at 11 P.M., where I held a midnight service; the church was filled to overflowing. On returning home a little after twelve the cornet was still going, but the notes were so thick and indistinct as to cause Dan Matthews to remark that the musician must have blown a quantity of whisky into the instrument, as he was struggling to get a tune out of it, but could not.

The next day telegrams of a contradictory nature were coming at short intervals. First we heard that Jameson had marched into Johannesburg unmolested, afterwards that he had been repulsed at Krugersdorp with heavy loss. We could get at nothing definite, the telegraph being still exclusively monopolised by Government. With regard to myself, I kept an open mind, and, partly to ascertain the truth of things, I left for Pretoria next morning at six o'clock by the coach. As showing the bitter race feeling evoked by the events of the last two days, I may mention that, at Kruger's Post, where we changed mules, I overheard a conversation between two burghers who were proceeding to the front. "I should like to meet twenty thousand 'Rooineks' with ten thousand Boers," said Burgher No. 1. "Oh, no!" replied No. 2, "you don't want so many as that; five thousand would be enough." "Yes," said No. 1; "five thousand would do; and we would teach them a lesson that would quiet them for ever." Proceeding on our way, we met a boy of about fifteen or so; the driver, Mr. du Plessis, stopped the coach to ask him "What news?" I could not understand all his reply, but a part of it was translated to me to this effect: "Our fathers fought the 'Rooineks,' and their sons will fight them now."

On reaching Lydenburg (about thirty-seven miles from Pilgrim's Rest) I found the place in a state of great commotion. Commandeering of horses and men had been briskly

My dear Rea

I am so sorry that I shall not be able to be present this afternoon at the presentation to Sir Jacob— It is only urgent business that keeps me away for my part know I am in strong sympathy with you in the matter.

What is wanted and one ... ...

... and words and an that stand coming from his heart though his life as from Ireland goes — conduct and words so widely different from that then and these used by other Boer Gentlemen in this country — what will form the true immortality when in course of the coming centuries those who have come to seek a home in our Republic with one thing and for watch.

I am yours faithfully
Ewald Esselen

LETTER FROM MR. EWALD ESSELEN,
LATE STATE ATTORNEY, Z.A.R.

going on, and the crisis was the general topic of conversation. Here, too, the telegraphic intelligence (or that part of it which the officials allowed the public to know) was unreliable, as the following quotations from my notes taken down at the time will show:—"Commandant Malan has met Jameson at Rustenburg, and taken all prisoners: four Maxims, one thousand rifles, and nine wagons of ammunition captured." Again, "England having offered the South African Republic help, it is reported that Jameson has surrendered." Another, "Lieutenant Scott and Trooper Dreyer reported wounded; the former's leg amputated; two Boers wounded." Further, "Lieutenant-Colonel Wollaston, who went out to meet and assist Jameson, is reported wounded, as also Sir John Willoughby; both lying in Krugersdorp Hospital." With regard to Colonel Wollaston going out to assist Jameson, there was no foundation whatever for the rumour. The gallant Colonel assured me, at an interview I had with him in Johannesburg, that the first intimation he had of the Uitlanders rising was his being called upon to find fifty men to protect life and property in Johannesburg, these men to do only police duty. I was advised in Lydenburg to obtain a passport from Government to secure me from molestation on my journey. This I accordingly did, the necessary document being provided by Mr. David Schoeman, Veld-Cornet. So bitter was the race feeling that Mr. —— was struck in the face, on his entering the club at Lydenburg, by a Boer, without any provocation being offered. Mr. ——, on the urgent advice of friends, did not retaliate. The commandeered burghers, some of whom I recognised as comrades in the late Malaboch campaign, were busy at the Landdrost's Court getting a supply of ammunition. The scene reminded me of that at Mr. Melt Marais' office in Pretoria, described at the beginning of this book but on a much smaller scale. There were about fifty men commandeered from the town, and these were to join the rest of the district commando, numbering altogether about five hundred men, at Pretoria. After calling on the Rev. J. Graham Reid, Rector of Lydenburg, Mrs. Bray, Mr. Thomas Rickard, and Mr. and Mrs. Steeple, I accepted the kind hospitality of Mr. Herbert Robinson for the night.

The following morning the commando formed up outside the club. Pretty well all the townspeople assembled to see them start. Just before the coach left for Machadodorp I heard three volleys fired, and away went the commando (mounted), bound also for Machadodorp. They arrived there before we did, and, on my asking at the hotel for a room for a few hours—until the departure of the train for Pretoria—the courteous and obliging proprietor told me he was at his wits' end, as he had one hundred of the mounted men to provide for. I was perforce obliged to while away the time by walking about Machadodorp. On my coming out of the hotel, after inquiring about the room, I saw that burghers were seated or lounging on every convenient spot, and I had not taken many steps when one of them called out to me, "Have you got your pass?" I took no notice at first, but on his repeating his question, I turned and asked him by what authority he made this demand. He replied, "I want to see your pass," which, however, I did not show him, and I walked away, whilst one of his companions remarked that I was "cheeky." I was the more anxious to avoid unnecessary altercation as at that moment I saw a lady (Miss Townsend) who had arrived from Johannesburg and was on her way to Pilgrim's Rest. Miss Townsend informed me that Johannesburg was in a state of intense excitement, many of the men there being armed, and all the mines closed down with the exception of two, and they were to be closed that day. She also said that the rumoured surrender of Dr. Jameson was still uncertain, and it was reported that the Black Watch from Cape Town and forces from Natal were on the border awaiting instructions; also that Sir Hercules

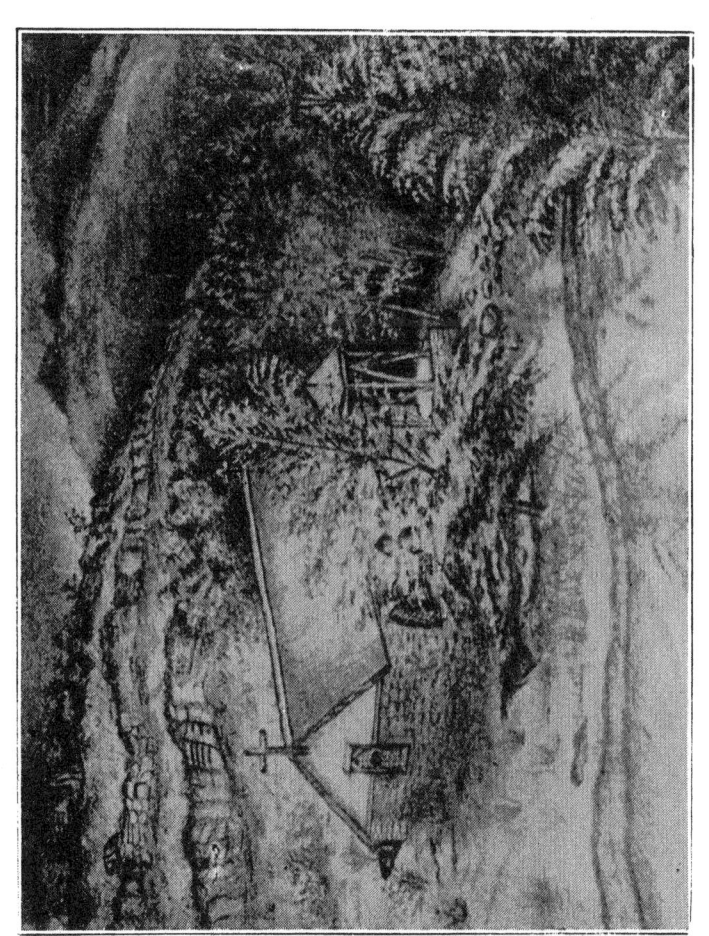

ST. MARY'S CHURCH, PILGRIM'S REST.
(From a sketch by Blythe E. Townsend.)

[To face page 222.

Robinson, Governor of Cape Colony, was expected to arrive at Pretoria for the purpose of mediating between the Uitlanders and the Boers. After dining at the hotel, I went up to the station in company with Mr. Bruce, who was on his way from the Clewer Estate to the Langlaagte Royal Gold-Mining Company, near Johannesburg. I reached Pretoria at seven the next morning, and, contrary to my expectations, found the railway station very quiet. The commandeered burghers who had come up in the same train at once mounted their horses and rode off.

I here received confirmation of the rumour anent Dr. Jameson's surrender. The prisoners were camped, closely guarded, on the racecourse, with the exception of Dr. Jameson, who was in the State prison, nobody being allowed to see him. The streets of Pretoria were being patrolled by armed men, in knots of twos and threes. From the railway station I went, at the invitation of the Bishop, to Bishop's Cote, the episcopal residence, where I had before been a guest on my return from the Malaboch expedition; during my stay there, the members of the Johannesburg Reform Committee, having surrendered to the Government in order to save the lives of Jameson and his men, were arrested by the Civil power and lodged in Pretoria Gaol.

On the evening of January 4th, the High Commissioner for South Africa, Sir Hercules Robinson (the late Lord Rosmead), arrived at Pretoria from Capetown. Although the streets were full of people, there was nothing of the nature of a popular demonstration in honour of his Excellency's arrival. An escort of the State Artillery rode close (very close) to his carriage in solemn silence, and I overheard a bystander remark that the procession was more like that of a funeral than anything else.

On arrival of the cavalcade at the Transvaal Hotel in Pretorius Street, a cheer was raised—a very half-hearted one —and it fell rather flat.

I experienced, as I always have, the greatest kindness from the Bishop and Mrs. Bousfield during my stay at Bishop's Cote.

On Tuesday, the 14th January, I left Pretoria for Johannesburg, and was accompanied by the Rev. R. J. P. Dunbar, who had also been a guest at Bishop's Cote.

We were driven to the railway station by the Bishop in his Lordship's carriage. My luggage was searched there to see that I was taking no arms or ammunition to the Rand, which was still in a state of ferment. I put up at Long's Hotel in Johannesburg, and I am indebted to Mr. and Mrs. Long, the worthy host and hostess, for much comfort during an exceptionally trying time.

Through the courtesy of the Rev. J. H. Williams, priest in charge of the mission at Roodepoort and Maraisburg, I had the privilege of conducting divine service at the latter place, where I renewed the acquaintance of many friends. I was the guest of Mr. and Mrs. Hellman, from whom I received much kindness during my ministry there in 1894. On Tuesday, January 21st, I visited the battlefield near Doornkop, about five miles from Maraisburg, being driven thither by Mr. Hellman, in company with Mr. John Muusse and Mr. Hellman's little son Max, who rode his favourite pony "Tom." We passed through Hamburg, turning off by Mr. Clarke's store and through the properties of the Kimberley-Roodepoort and the Ida Gold-Mining Companies.

We observed, *en route*, on a board exhibited outside an hotel, a strange sign, thus : " Randevoux Hotel," and could not understand the idea of such a sign, except that the proprietor may have been anxious to display his ignorance of *la langue Française*, or advertise his aptitude for making puns.

Mr. Muusse informed me that the battle was fought near Brink's Farm, Vlakfontein, close to the Doornkop Boundary, but not actually at Doornkop. He and Mr. Edwards, of Maraisburg, arrived on the scene just at the close of the

PILGRIM'S REST MINING CAMP (FROM THE WEST), DISTRICT LYDENBURG

battle, whilst the white flags were still flying, and he saw only three dead troopers. It was, he said, a ghastly sight; and on his asking some of the wounded how they fared, the reply was that they were having every necessary attention. He also saw eight dead horses within a radius of about ten yards, and two dead mules close to Brink's homestead. (The bodies of the horses and mules were still there on the occasion of our visit.) A policeman of Florida, named Swanepoel, who met Muusse, told him that one of the Dutchmen was so overjoyed at the result of the battle that he appeared to lose his self-control, and danced about to such an extent that his gun went off, killing him on the spot.

The Battle of Doornkop.

The following account of the battle—the last great struggle, *vi et armis*, between the two white races of South Africa—I take from the Pretoria *Press* of Thursday, 4th January.

"It would seem that on Monday (1st January, 1896) a strong body of the Chartered Company's troops crossed the Transvaal border and passed through Malmani, swerving to the right to keep such a direction as to be able to strike the high road between Blaauw Bank and Johannesburg, at a spot in the neighbourhood of Krugersdorp. It may be said that, during the march, due military preparations were taken against surprise; and in order to leave the rugged tract of country to the left the troops took their way over the undulating uplands, Dr. Jameson in person commanding the columns, assisted by Sir John Willoughby, Major Gray, and other officers. The Burgher forces were supposed to be intrenched among the Coomby ridges near Rietspruit. The troops were marching in double column with flanking parties, advance and rear guards.

Krugersdorp, 2.50 *p.m.*—Almost at this moment I (war correspondent) caught sight of them, surveying them from the rise; dense bodies of Burghers riding in open order loomed up on the ridges away to the left front, and the whole of the contending forces were brought up within Martini distance of each other. The sudden appearance of the Burghers was evidently no surprise to the troopers, who pluckily though venturously marched on, through the open valley, commanded on each side and in front by rocky ridges. At 4 P.M., the troopers opened fire upon the position of the Burghers, apparently intending to presently carry the position by storm. Commandant H. Malan meanwhile with his division, supported by contingents of the Pretoria District Burghers under Veld-Cornets Glas and Roos, numbering about five hundred, had occupied and strongly intrenched themselves within the confines of the Otto Battery. His position was well chosen. Presently the Maxims opened fire, followed by Gardners, their shrapnel fire being a very bad one. However, plunging into the position, they threw up myriads of small stones, thereby wounding one Botha, of the Krugersdorp Division. About thirty of the British South African troops charged at the same time the back of the column, halting on the crest of the ridge on our left front, where they were checked. Seven fell, five wounded and two killed. The wounded troopers were F. Dreyer, J. Maclaughlan, F. Mostyn, B. MacCrackam, and M. Den. The Burghers wounded were (of the Potchefstroom Contingent) Klas Cronje, seriously; (Krugersdorp Contingent) Botha, slightly.

Again the little handful of troopers charged, but the horses were seen to fall, and men to topple from their saddles, the unerring rifle aim of the Boer being too much for the advancing column. Most of the dismounted troopers took flight, throwing their arms away, and that which had shown a brave front before became a fugitive crowd. Desultory fire on both sides then ensued, and I did not fail to observe that the day had been decidedly in favour of the Boers. The following are the names of the B.S.A. officers and troopers who were captured and handed over to the Landdrost that evening: Captain Charles Frederic Lindsell, Lieutenant Henry Farquhar Scott, Dr. William Henry Farmer; John Hall Hill, George John Wetherell, Richard Barry Jupp, Philip Lancelot Rolleston, Simon Gettiffe, Percy Solomon, Percy Charles Stevenson, Charles McGowan, John Calderwood, Edwin Abbott, George White, Edward Mansfield, Edward Rogers, Lowen Ernest Mageen, Benjamin William Webb, Henry Collins, Bell, Joseph George King.

The rest of the invading troops then retreated towards Randfontein.

Krugersdorp, Thursday, 10 *a.m.*—The attack on Krugersdorp having been repelled in the night, the troops retired on Randfontein, an hour (about six miles) to the south of Krugersdorp, and there remained. This, it would seem, was a measure which Sir John Willoughby had good reason to follow, for his pressing need of food and reinforcements made it vital for him to push on rapidly, so as to reach Johannesburg at an early hour this morning. Commandants Malan, Trichardt, and Potgieter left for Randfontein, taking with them about 1500 men. Again the column marched forward, but near Prinsloo's farm the Burgher forces made a determined stand, killing one trooper, besides capturing a Maxim gun and an ammunition wagon, with fifteen cases of ammunition. Our (Dutch) losses were two killed throughout the running skirmish; the troopers, however, suffered severely; as the fight developed, horses and men fell frequently. On riding over the ground subsequently by the line of march the sight was really sickening. Strong men lay low; here a cheek had been pierced by a bullet, there a man had fallen to the ground with outstretched arms and glassy eye, soon to lie silent for ever. Still pursuing the line of march, the now famous farm of Hendrik Brink was reached, where the troopers at once established themselves. The flanking heights were immediately occupied by Burghers, and a cordon of armed men was drawn around the plucky though misguided band.

While this was being done Captain Erasmus and a detachment of the State Artillery arrived, and took up a strong position on a kopje to the north of the farm, from whence he proceeded to shell the farmhouse outbuildings with four Krupp guns, besides sending in an occasional Maxim fusilade. To this no reply was given. It was a sign of import, for cannon fire was scarcely developed when flags of truce were displayed, and by 11 A.M. Dr. Jameson and his officers, among whom were Sir John Willoughby, Captain Munro, Lieutenants Mageen, Wood, and Hoare, and the whole of the Malmani column, consisting of about five hundred men with eight Maxims, two Gardners, and five to six hundred rifles, revolvers, etc., had surrendered to Commandants H. Malan and P. Cronje."

The casualties were as follows:—

OFFICIAL LIST.

British South Africa Company. Killed: Captain Barry (died in hospital); Corporals Beard and Maree; Troopers Lamb, Shippard, Still, Coghill, Black, Forster, Myers, Betsoe, Edwards, Fraser, Wüd (died in hospital), Hutchinson, Stone, Reeland, Hennesy. Wounded: Captain C. J. Coventry; Sergeants B. McCracken, E. G. Barnes; Corporals F. Dreyer, D. Fraser, S. Burrows; Troopers William McLaughlan, F. Mostyn, M. Den, F. M. Brooke, G. McVetty, F. Stannard, G. Pomeroy, H. A. Callenan, G. A. Palmer, A. M. Rowlley, T. R. Lynn, D. M. Fyvie, L. H. Stapleton, G. Potter, G. R. Payne, H. C. Gibbs, H. Marchant, S. Bruce, F. Nickson, E. A. Berry, H. Beadon, G. Wilson, B. R. Philbrick, F. W. Brown, F. A. Hays, Kolonel Grey, G. B. Lamb, Cazalet, Lennard Garringe.

Burgher forces. Killed: S. van Tonder (accident by Boers), A. Potgieter (accident by Boers), P. P. Venter, G. Jacobs, D. McDonald. Wounded: Klas Cronje, B. van der Berg, Philip van der Walt, C. P. Roos (sick), Van der Merwe, D. Strijdom, O'Grady, P. Bezuidenhout (accident).

So ended the battle of Doornkop; the result (unhappy or otherwise, according to the reader's political opinions) was in a great measure due to the exhaustion of men and horses, consequent upon the great haste with which a column of about five hundred armed men, with big guns, ammunition wagons, and complete outfit had *rushed* (there is no other term) from the time of their entering South African Republic territory to the fatal *dénouement*, a distance of one hundred and ninety miles, in the incredible time of two days.

As I have already mentioned (page 224), I visited the battlefield, accompanied by Mr. Hellman and party, on January 21st. On our arrival at the scene of action, we first visited the grave of the troopers who fell; the illustration opposite page 238 gives a good idea of the spot, and is from a photograph. The trench is about thirty feet long, three feet broad, and four feet deep. Only about eight feet of this excavation is used as a grave, and that part is filled in with earth and boulders; at the time of our visit, there were indications of withered wreaths of flowers that some tender-hearted people had placed there. As we alighted, an old Boer, by the name of Scholtz, came up and offered for sale a battered felt hat which he said had belonged to one of the burgher force. The price he asked was two shillings and sixpence, but we did no business.

The hat was dirty and greasy, and might or might not have belonged to one of the warriors. Mr. Scholtz was very loquacious, and Mr. Hellman remarked: "He can talk—he's like perpetual motion." A good deal of what the old Boer said was "invented for the occasion," with the object of doing business. I saw altogether the bodies of twenty-five dead horses, and it was a noticeable fact that most of them were wounded in or near the head; a great many vultures had been busy with the carrion, and bones (of horses) were scattered all around.

We instituted a search for mementos, and succeeded in finding part of a Lee-Metford ramrod, a cartridge case, a necktie, and a bullet. A picture of these is given opposite

CHURCH OF ST. JOHN THE EVANGELIST, LYDENBURG.
(*Photographed by G. A. Robertson.*)

[*To face page* 228.

page 246; the feathers shown are some that fell from the many vultures just mentioned.

Scholtz's vocabulary was simply inexhaustible; among other yarns, he told us that nine Boers advanced from the main body of the burghers and utterly routed Jameson's column; after this, "Thermopylæ" must take a back seat, though this last bit of information was not volunteered by Scholtz. Mr. Muusse pointed out to us the place where a shell had struck and burst. Stones and earth had been flung on all sides in wildest confusion by the force of the explosion, and quite a trench had been ploughed up in the ground.

On returning from the battlefield we passed through Florida, a suburb of Johannesburg, and on reaching Maraisburg Mr. Hellman was good enough to give me two loaded cartridges, one a Lee-Metford and the other a Maxim (see illustration), which he had himself extracted from Dr. Jameson's bandolier, in Pretoria.

I left Maraisburg that day and returned to Johannesburg, and from there proceeded to Pretoria *en route* to Pilgrim's Rest.

In connection with the scare at Johannesburg, women and children, and even men, left (what seemed to them) the doomed city in hundreds; many going to Capetown *viâ* Vereeniging, and others *viâ* the Netherlands and Natal Railways to various centres in the latter Colony.

A train crowded with these refugees left Charlestown (the Natal border township) at 10.15 A.M. on Tuesday, the 31st December, 1895. At a point near Glencoe Junction, in Natal, at about 2.30 P.M., a Netherlands carriage left the rails and ran into the bank at a curve; the remainder of the Netherlands carriages ran on, completely somersaulting and smashing the woodwork to atoms. The result was appalling. Thirty-nine dead bodies were taken from the

230   APPENDIX

débris, while about the same number suffered frightful injuries. The dead were torn and disfigured by the flying splinters of wood and iron—in some cases beyond recognition.

It is beyond the powers of pen to describe the heart-rending scenes enacted on the Biggarsberg on that New Year's Eve. Never before in the history of South African railways has occurred such a catastrophe. May such never happen again!

New Year's Day, 1896, was ushered in with the rattle of Maxims and rifles and the crash of railway rolling stock, dealing death and destruction around, the saddest and gloomiest New Year's Day in the annals of South Africa.

Subsequent Events.

The trial of the Reformers took place in Pretoria on the 24th April and following days, Judge Gregorowski, of the Orange Free State, having been especially appointed by the Transvaal Government to try the case.

The names of the prisoners were:—Messrs. Lionel Phillips, George Farrar, Francis Rhodes, John Hays Hammond, James Percy Fitzpatrick, Robert Mitchell, Walter Edward Hudson, William St. John Carr, Fritz Mosenthal, William Thomas Frederic Davis, John Andrew Roger, Hans Sauer, David Peter Duirs, Alfred Peter Hillier, Andrew Mackie Niven, Charles Mullins, William Henry Somerset Bell, Edward Philip Solomon, Alfred Leonard Lawley, Victor Michel Clement, Charles Albert Garland, Frederic Rodney Lingham, Robert George Fricker, Walter B. Davis, Philip du Bois, Henry Charles Hull, Douglas Flemmer Gilfillan, Herbert Evan Becher, Joseph Storey Curtis, Henry Brown Marshall, Charles Butters, Francis Henry Spencer, Thomas Mein, Alfred Brown, John Linda Williams, William

EXCITEMENT IN JOHANNESBURG, OUTSIDE THE GOLDFIELDS BUILDINGS.

[*To face page* 230.

Hampden Brodie, Frederick Gray, Charles Llewellyn Anderson, William Beachey Head, John Mortimer Buckland, Albert Raphael Goldring, Harold Fairbrother Strange, Edward Oliver Hutchinson, William Goddard, Solomon Barnato Joel, Abe Bailey, John George Auret, H. A. Rogers, Drummond Mils Dunbar, John Lace, Gordon Sandilands, Roland Bettington, Willem van Hulsteyn, Henry Bettelheim, William Hosken, Max Langerman, Samuel Watson Jameson, George Richards, Frederick H. Hamilton, James Weston Leonard, Charles Arthur Claud Tremeer, James Donaldson, A. Woolls Sampson.

They were charged thus:—Firstly, that they wrongfully, unlawfully, and with a hostile intention to disturb, injure, or bring into danger the independence or safety of the South African Republic, treated, conspired, agreed with and urged Leander Starr Jameson, an alien, residing without the boundaries of the Republic, to come into the territory at the head of, and with, an armed and hostile troop, and to make a hostile invasion, and to march through to Johannesburg. Secondly, they gave, or attempted to give, the aforementioned Jameson information as to the state of defences at Johannesburg, and had armed troops ready to assist, and sent assistance to him, and subsequently by seditious speeches endeavoured to persuade and induce the people there to stand by the afore-mentioned Jameson, in his hostile invasion, and had provided him with provisions, horses, and forage. Thirdly, for having distributed, or caused to be distributed, Maxims, guns, other weapons, arms and ammunition, and enrolled men, and formed them into military corps; and for having erected earthworks and other fortifications. Fourthly, for having arrogated to themselves the functions and powers belonging to the authorities of the South African Republic, and by violence and threats, compelled the police of Johannesburg to leave the public squares and streets, and for having formed their own police corps, and provided it with guns and other arms, and appointed as head of that corps, Andrew Trimble, and entrusted him with jurisdiction in police cases, in virtue whereof the afore-mentioned Andrew Trimble had passed sentence, and caused it to be carried out.

Counsel for the prosecution were: Dr. Coster (State Attorney), Messrs. W. H. Lohman, F. E. T. Klause, and J. K. Hummel. For the defence: Mr. Wessels, aided by Messrs. B. Sauer, A. Muller, and J. de Villiers. Mr. I. Rose-Innes, Q.C., watched the case on behalf of the Imperial Government; Mr. R. P. Solomon appeared to watch the case on behalf of Messrs. Phillips, Farrar, Hammond, and Fitzpatrick specially. Mr. Dixon also represented Mr. Herbert Becher specially.

The pleas were:—Messrs. Phillips, Farrar, Rhodes, and Hammond guilty of High Treason on the first count. The others pleaded guilty to *gekwetste majesteit* (sedition), in that, they acknowledged wrongfully and unlawfully to have distributed guns and other arms and ammunition, and enrolled persons and formed them into military corps, and for having erected earthworks and other fortifications, as set forth in the third count, but with no hostile intention to disturb the safety of the Republic. They also acknowledged having committed the acts as specified in the fourth count (with the exception of the removal of the State police and the entrusting of judicial decision to Andrew Trimble), but with no hostile intention to disturb the safety of the Republic.

The trial caused great excitement in Johannesburg. Between the chains it was the sole topic of discussion, and information was eagerly looked for from Pretoria. After the first intimation that a plea of guilty had been given, the most absurd rumours were floated, one being to the effect that the ringleaders had been heavily fined and banished from the country.

There was an immense rush of work at the telegraph office,

THE OFFICES OF THE REFORM COMMITTEE.

[*To face page* 232.

APPENDIX

and, in consequence, private messages from Pretoria were delayed for several hours.

Mr. Wessels informed the Court that the accused wished to hand in several declarations which had been made and signed by them. Having handed in a Dutch copy of the original declarations made by Messrs. Lionel Phillips, George Farrar, Francis Rhodes, and John Hays Hammond, Mr. Wessels read the following translation in English :—

"For a number of years endeavours have been made to obtain by constitutional means the redress of the grievances under which the Uitlander population labour. The new-comers asked for no more than is conceded to immigrants by all the other governments in South Africa, under which every man may on reasonable conditions become a citizen of the State, whilst here alone a policy is pursued by which the first settlers retain the exclusive right of government.

Petitions supported by the signatures of some 40,000 men were ignored, and when it was found that we could not get a fair and reasonable hearing—that provisions already deemed obnoxious and unfair were being made more stringent, and that we were being debarred for ever from obtaining the rights which in other countries are freely granted, it was then realised that we would never get redress until we should make a demonstration of force to support our claims.

Certain provision was made regarding arms and ammunition, and a letter was written to Dr. Jameson, in which he was asked to come to our aid, under certain circumstances.

On December 26th, 1895, the Uitlanders' manifesto was published, and it was then our intention to make a final appeal for redress, at the public meeting which was to have been held on the 6th January. In consequence of matters that came to our knowledge, we sent, on December 26th, Major Heany by train, *viâ* Kimberley, and Captain Holden across country, to forbid any movement on Dr. Jameson's part.

On the afternoon of Monday, 30th December, we learnt, from Government sources, that Dr. Jameson had crossed the frontier. We assumed that he had come in good faith to help us, probably misled by some of the exaggerated rumours which were then in circulation. We were convinced, however, that the Government and the burghers would not in the excitement of the moment believe that we had not invited Dr. Jameson in, and there was no course open to us but to prepare to defend ourselves if attacked, and, at the same time, to spare no effort to effect a peaceful settlement. It became necessary to form an organisation for the protection of the town and the maintenance of order; since, in the excitement caused by the news of Dr. Jameson's coming, serious disturbances would be likely to occur, and it was evident that the Government organisation could not deal with the people without serious risk of conflict.

The Reform Committee was formed on Monday night, the 30th December, and it was intended to include such men of influence as cared to associate themselves with the movement. The object with which it was formed is best shown in its first notice, viz. :—

'Notice is hereby given that this Committee adheres to the National Union Manifesto, and reiterates its desire to maintain the independence of the Republic. The fact that rumours are in course of circulation to the effect that a force has crossed the Bechuanaland border renders it necessary to take active steps for the defence of Johannesburg, and preservation of order. The Committee earnestly desire that the inhabitants should refrain from taking any action which can be construed as an overt act of hostility against the Government.

By order of the Committee,
J. PERCY FITZPATRICK.'

The evidence taken at the preliminary examination will show that order was maintained by this Committee during a time of intense excitement, and through the action of the Committee no aggressive steps whatever were taken against the Government, but, on the contrary, the property of the Government was protected, and its officials were not interfered with.

It is our firm belief that had no such Committee been formed, the intense excitement caused by Dr. Jameson's entry would have brought about utter chaos in Johannesburg.

It has been alleged that we armed natives.

This is absolutely untrue, and is disposed of by the fact that during the crisis upwards of 20,000 white men applied to us for arms and we were unable to get them.

On Tuesday morning, 31st December, we hoisted the flag of the South African Republic, and every man bound himself to maintain the Independence of the Republic. On the same day the Government withdrew its police voluntarily from the town, and we preserved perfect order.

During the evening of that day, Messrs. Marais and Malan presented themselves as delegates from the Executive Council. They came (to use their own words) to offer us the olive-branch, and they told us that if we would send a deputation to Pretoria to meet a Commission appointed by the Government, we should probably obtain 'practically all that we asked for in the manifesto.'

Our deputation met the Government Commission, consisting of Chief Justice Kotzé, Judge Ameshoff, and Mr. Kock, member of the Executive.

[*To face page* 234.

THE LATE LORD ROSMEAD (SIR HERCULES ROBINSON),
H.M.'S HIGH COMMISSIONER FOR SOUTH AFRICA.

On our behalf our deputation frankly avowed knowledge of Jameson's presence on the border, and of his intention by arrangement with us to assist us in case of extremity.

With the full knowledge of this arrangement, with the knowledge that we were in arms and agitating for our rights, the Government Commission handed to us a resolution by the Executive Council, of which the following is the purport:—

'Sir Hercules Robinson has offered his services, with a view to a peaceful settlement. The Government of the South African Republic has accepted his offer. Pending his arrival, no hostile steps will be taken against Johannesburg, providing Johannesburg takes no hostile action against the Government in terms of a certain proclamation recently passed by the President, and the grievances will be earnestly considered.'

We acted in perfect good faith with the Government, believing it to be their desire, as it was ours, to avert bloodshed, and believing it to be their intention to give us the redress which was implied in the 'earnest consideration of grievances.'

There can be no better evidence of our earnest endeavour to repair what we regarded as a mistake on the part of Dr. Jameson than the following offer which our deputation authorised by resolution of the Committee laid before the Government Commission :—

'If the Government will permit Dr. Jameson to come to Johannesburg unmolested, the Committee will guarantee, with their persons, if necessary, that he will leave again peacefully as soon as possible.'

We faithfully carried out the agreement that we should commit no act of hostility against the Government; we ceased all active operations for the defence of the town against any attack, and we did everything in our power to prevent any collision with the burghers—an attempt in which our efforts were happily successful. On the telegraphic advice of the result of the interview of the deputation with the Government Commission, we dispatched Mr. Lace, a member of our Committee, as an escort to the courier carrying High Commissioner's dispatch to Dr. Jameson, in order to assure ourselves that the dispatch would reach its destination.

On the following Saturday, January 4th, the High Commissioner arrived in Pretoria.

On Monday, the 6th, the following telegram was sent to us :—

'PRETORIA, 6th Jan., 1896.

From H.M. AGENT. To REFORM COMMITTEE, Johannesburg.

6th Jan.—I am directed to inform you that the High Commissioner met President, the Executive, and the Judges to-day.

The President announced the decision of the Government to be that Johannesburg must lay down its arms unconditionally, as a condition precedent to a discussion and consideration of grievances. The High

Commissioner endeavoured to obtain some indication of the steps which would be taken in the event of disarmament, but without success, it being intimated that the Government had nothing more to say on this subject than had already been embodied in the President's proclamation.

The High Commissioner inquired whether any decision had been come to as regards the disposal of prisoners, and received a reply in the negative. The President said that as his burghers to the number of eight thousand had been collected, and could not be asked to remain indefinitely, he must request reply Yes or No to this ultimatum within twenty-four hours. Witness, J. DE WET, H.M. Agent.'

On the following day, Sir Jacobus de Wet, H.M. Agent, met us in Committee, and handed to us the following wire from H. E. the High Commissioner :—

From HIGH COMMISSIONER, Pretoria.

To SIR JACOBUS DE WET, Johannesburg.

Received, Johannesburg, 7.36 A.M., 7th Jan., 1896. Urgent. You should inform Johannesburg people that I consider that if they lay down their arms they will be acting loyally and honourably, and that if they do not comply with my request they forfeit all claim to sympathy from Her Majesty's Government and from British subjects throughout the world, as the lives of Jameson and prisoners are practically in their hands.

On this, and assurances given in Executive Council resolution, we laid down our arms on the 6th, 7th, and 8th January. On the 9th we were arrested, and have since been under arrest in Pretoria, a period of three and a half months.

We admit responsibility for action taken by us. We frankly avowed it at the time of the negotiations with the Government when we were informed that the services of the High Commissioner had been accepted with a view to a peaceful settlement.

We submit that we kept the faith in every detail in the arrangement with the Government, that we did all that was humanly possible to protect both the State and Dr. Jameson from the consequence of his action; that we have committed no breach of the law which was not known to Government at the time that the earnest consideration of our grievances was promised. We can now only lay the bare facts before the Court and submit to the judgment that may be passed upon us."

With reference to the remaining fifty-nine accused, Mr. Wessels read their declaration as follows :—

"We have heard the statement made by Mr. Lionel Phillips, and we

RESIDENCE OF MR. H. HELLMAN, MARAISBURG.

[*To face page* 236.

freely agree with what he has said as regards the objects with which the Reform Committee was formed.

Since the formation of the Committee we have worked with these gentlemen, and the only object all had in view was to use their utmost endeavours to avert bloodshed, but at the same time to endeavour to obtain a redress of what we considered very serious grievances."

Advocate Wessels also admitted, on behalf of Colonel Francis Rhodes, that he was "Toad," mentioned in one of the telegrams produced to the Court.

The case in defence of the accused was opened by Mr. Wessel, the senior Counsel for the Reformers, in a speech which lasted exactly two hours. The learned Counsel urged that the milder form of punishment for *gekwetste majesteit* be inflicted. The legislature of the country had defined the punishment with regard to the crime above referred to in the 33rd Article of the Grondwet. In that article it is enacted that persons who conspire with any foreign Power for the purpose of bringing the State into subjection to such Power, are liable to a fine of five hundred rixdollars (a rixdollar is one shilling and sixpence) and banishment, and if he returned he is liable to the punishment of outlawry. Mr. Wessels contended that although the capital punishment for high treason was still in force in the Republic, according to the old Roman-Dutch Law, yet that law was now obsolete and could not be applied in this case. He referred to the past work of the four leaders in warm, eulogistic terms, and finished his brilliant speech by earnestly appealing for clemency. He assured the Court that if the sharp edge of the sword were used the result would be eternal unrest; but that if the flat end be employed, the peace and safety of the South African Republic would be assured.

The State Attorney then rose and stated that the law should be rigorously applied. The only punishment for high treason, as laid down by Van der Linden, was death and confiscation of property.

He requested the Court to inflict the highest punishment on the accused, according to the old Roman-Dutch Law. This impassioned appeal, after Counsel for the defence had closed his case, caused quite a sensation. It was felt that the pressing for inflicting the capital sentence and confiscation of property was in acute contrast to the general plea of guilty on the part of all the accused, and many members of the Reform Committee regretted that the general plea had been made.

The Judge then summed up the whole case. Everyone strained forward in anxiety to catch the learned Judge's remarks as he deliberately read his carefully prepared speech. At its close a hushed expectancy followed, and, amid a painful silence, Messrs. Lionel Phillips, George Farrar, John Hays Hammond, and Colonel F. Rhodes were conducted from among the body of their *confrères* to a dock brought in for that purpose. They were asked one by one whether they had anything to say why sentence of death should not be passed upon them, and they each replied "No."

The death sentence was then pronounced by the Judge upon Mr. Lionel Phillips, and, in turn, upon Mr. George Farrar, Colonel F. Rhodes, and Mr. John Hays Hammond, each prisoner taking up his position at the end of the dock nearest the Judge, and bowing reverently as the solemn words, "And may Almighty God have mercy on your soul," were pronounced.

Many of the ladies present—relatives and friends of the condemned—were most deeply affected, and had to be removed from the Court in a fainting condition. Mrs. Lionel Phillips especially was terribly upset at hearing the sentence.

The prisoners themselves heard their penalty pronounced without flinching.

On few such men in their station of life, or for such an offence, has the extreme penalty of the law been pronounced

TROOPERS' GRAVE AT DOORNKOP.

[*To face page* 238.

in recent times, and the feeling of all present was that the occasion was both an exceptional and painful experience.

After the four condemned had been removed from the dock, the Judge pronounced sentence on the remaining fifty-nine. The sentence of the Court upon each of these was two years' imprisonment, together with a fine of £2000, with three years' banishment from the State after the period of incarceration, the alternative of the fine being another year's imprisonment.

The prisoners were then brought out, and, forming themselves into line four and five abreast, were escorted to the Pretoria Gaol under a strong detachment of the State artillery. While *en route* the majority of them seized the opportunity of regaling themselves with the fragrant weed. Members of the artillery on foot surrounded the column of prisoners, the mounted men of the corps being on the outside.

The whole made up an imposing cavalcade, and the scene was, perhaps, the most unique spectacle ever witnessed in Pretoria.

The news regarding the severity of the sentences was received in Johannesburg with the greatest excitement and concern, and the scene between the chains was one that has not been paralleled since the late crisis.

A meeting of the members of the Stock Exchange was hurriedly summoned, when it was resolved to close the Exchange, and a cablegram was at once dispatched to the London Stock Exchange soliciting the assistance of the members to exert their influence in trying to obtain a mitigation of the heavy sentences passed upon the Reform Committee. All the places of amusement and business houses were closed.

Mr. B. I. Barnato, acting in his capacity of Life Governor of the De Beers Consolidated Mine, Kimberley, telegraphed to the head office, instructing the secretary to close down the diamond mines for one day, as a mark of sympathy with the condemned prisoners in Pretoria. Mr. Barnato also threatened to close down all mining properties, and sell out all the landed properties belonging to the firm, a threat, I am happy to state, which was never carried into effect; had it been, the consequences would have been terrible: a large number of workmen would have been thrown out of employment, and the gold production of the Rand materially decreased, thus reducing, though indirectly, the revenue of the State.

Mr. Barnato, although highly indignant at the severity of the sentences, soon saw that to pursue such a course would tend to deter rather than attain his ends, and, grasping the gravity of the situation, took a more sensible and rational view, and set to work in right earnest by interviewing the President and other high officials of the State, in order to obtain the release of his friends; indeed (be it to his credit), he left no stone unturned until he had gained his heart's desire. His efforts were at last crowned with success, and, no man gripped the hands of the Reformers (upon their discharge) with a bigger heart, or with more thorough genuineness, than Mr. B. I. Barnato. Well might he be banqueted and held in honour; for, chiefly through his exertions, the members of the late Reform Committee owe their liberty of to-day.

Much indignation and uneasiness were evinced in Kimberley, Durban, Natal, and Port Elizabeth; and Maritzburg, following the example of Johannesburg, closed the Stock Exchange as a mark of sympathy.

Petitions from every part of South Africa were signed, praying the Government and Executive to exercise their prerogative of mercy and commute the death sentence. This was accordingly done. The following morning (April 29th) at 9.30 A.M., the Executive met and decided not to carry out the capital sentence.

REFUGEES FLEEING FROM JOHANNESBURG.

[*To face page* 240.

APPENDIX

Petitions still flowed rapidly in, and it is only fair to mention that the burghers were as anxious as anybody to obtain a further mitigation of punishment, and freely signed their names.

The commuted sentence on the four leaders was imprisonment for fifteen years and banishment for life.

In the meantime, active agitation had been going on for a general commutation of sentences passed on the remainder of the prisoners.

The feeling being that this was an opportunity for the display of mercy, and this feeling was accentuated by the sad suicide of Mr. Frederick Gray (while in gaol), whose mind had become quite unhinged, through the terrible strain the trial had involved, and the hardships of prison life.

On the 30th May, 1896, fifty-six of the Reformers then in the Pretoria Goal (exclusive of the four leaders) were liberated, on the payment of a fine of £2000 each, and a written guarantee of abstention from political intrigue on pain of banishment from the State. The other two (Messrs. Sampson and Davis) refused to sign the guarantee of abstention from politics, and consequently remained in gaol. They were subsequently unconditionally pardoned by President Kruger, on the occasion of Her Majesty Queen Victoria's Diamond Jubilee, 1897.

Amongst those present at the prison gates, to greet the released Reformers, was the Right Rev. the Bishop of Pretoria, who proposed three cheers for the President, which was heartily and vociferously taken up by the crowd.

The agitation for a further mitigation of the sentence passed on the four leaders was by no means at an end. Petition after petition still poured in upon the Government, until it was resolved by the two English colonies to send a deputation to Pretoria of all Mayors of boroughs (numbering nearly 200), and to present the petitions in person to the Government. Before, however, they were presented, and whilst the Mayoral deputation was in Pretoria, Messrs. Lionel

Phillips, George Farrar, John Hays Hammond, and Colonel Francis Rhodes, on the 11th June, emerged from the prison gates, free men, after paying a fine of £25,000 each, and signing a declaration similar to that signed by their *confrères*.

Colonel Rhodes, however, as an officer of the Imperial Government, declined to give such a pledge; and, after the payment of the £25,000, was escorted to the border of the Republic at Mafeking, and at once proceeded to the assistance of the Chartered forces then at war with the insurgent Matabele and Mashona.

* * * * * *

The trial of Dr. Jameson and his five companions concerned in the raid upon the Transvaal was opened on Monday, the 20th July, 1896, before Lord Russell, Mr. Baron Pollock, and Mr. Justice Hawkins, in the Court of the Lord Chief Justice.

The defendants were indicted under the Foreign Enlistment Act, and their names were: Dr. Leander Starr Jameson, Major Sir John Christopher Willoughby, Colonel the Hon. Henry Frederick White, Colonel Raleigh Grey, Major the Hon. Robert White, and Major the Hon. Charles John Coventry.

The Attorney-General (Sir Richard Webster), the Solicitor-General (Sir R. B. Finlay), Mr. Sutton, Mr. C. Matthews, Mr. Horace Avory, and Mr. Rawlinson appeared for the prosecution; Sir Edward Clarke, Q.C., Mr. Carson, Q.C., Mr. C. F. Gill, Mr. A. Lyttleton, and Mr. Howard Spensley, junior, for the defendants Jameson and Willoughby, H. F. White, and R. White; and Sir F. Lockwood, Q.C., Mr. J. P. Wallis, and Mr. J. Roskill for the defendants Grey and Coventry. Mr. A. Cohen, Q.C., Mr. Saunders, and Mr. Felix Cassel held a watching brief on behalf of the South African Republic.

Before the special jury was sworn, Sir Edward Clarke moved that the indictment be quashed on technical grounds,

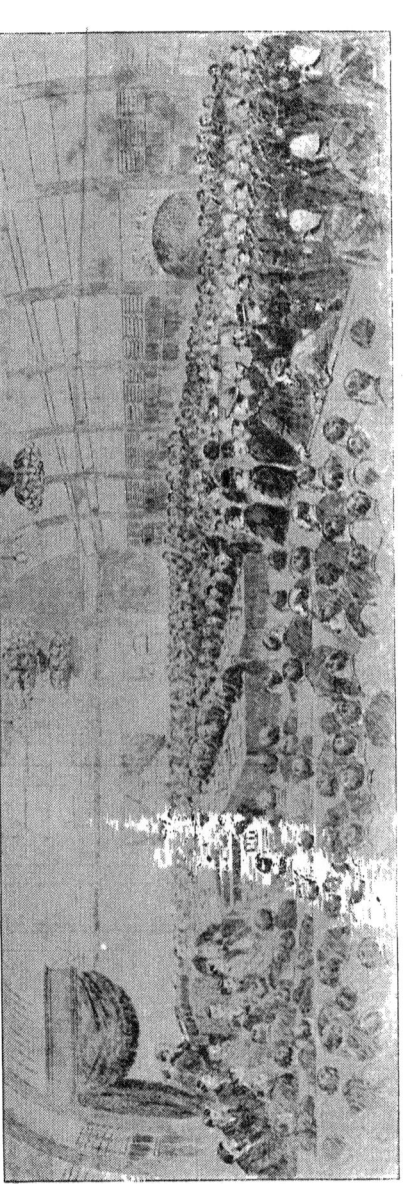

THE GREAT REFORM TRIAL AT PRETORIA.—THE SCENE IN COURT.

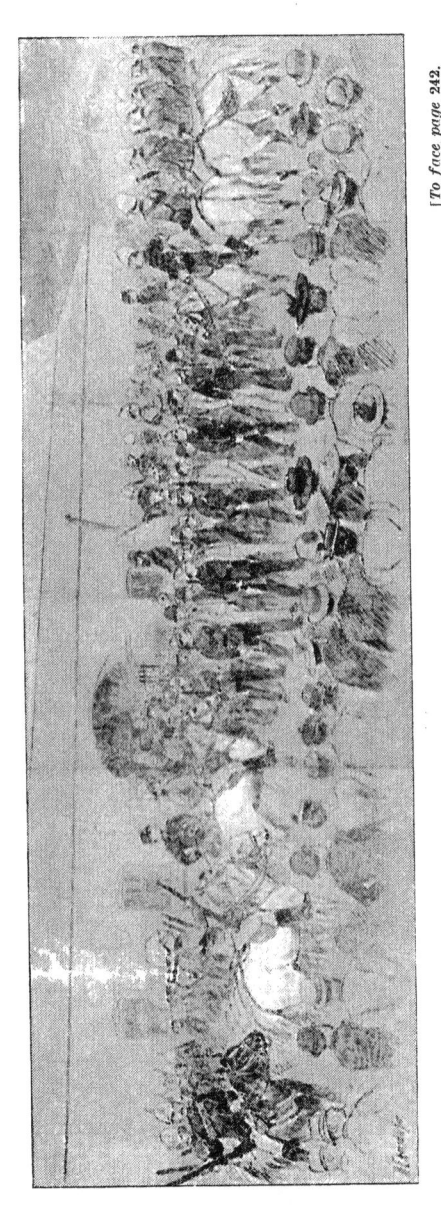

THE GREAT REFORM TRIAL AT PRETORIA.—AFTER THE SENTENCE, MARCHING TO GAOL.

[*To face page* 242.

that the Enlistment Act did not apply to British Bechuanaland, giving authorities and precedents.

He further contended that no force was fitted out at Mafeking, and that there was no idea of any hostile intent against a foreign State, and that the Reformers' appeal for aid justified Dr. Jameson. His speech lasted for two hours.

Sir Richard Webster replied, urging that the indictment was perfectly in order. He admitted that it was necessary to prove that the Act was in force at the time and at the place where the offences were committed, but this was sufficiently implied in the general terms of the indictment. He maintained that both Mafeking and Pitsani were under British law, and he ridiculed the idea of the raid being of a peaceful character. Evidence, he said, showed that it was premeditated.

The Lord Chief Justice delivered judgment the following day on the objections to the indictment raised by Sir Edward Clarke. He said they had come to the conclusion that none of the objections applied to the indictment as a whole, or to any count in the indictment.

It was said, first, that it was not stated that the place in which it was alleged the illegal preparations for the expedition had taken place was within Her Majesty's dominions in which the Act was in operation. He could not doubt that the language of the indictment stated reasonably and intelligently that the defendants were engaged in a place within Her Majesty's dominions in which the Act of 1870 was in operation; and were engaged in the preparation of an expedition which would be an offence against the law. The second objection was, that the counts were bad because they did not state the fact of the proclamation of the Act. He thought that that was an objection which was not valid. Further, it was not necessary to state that the defendants were subjects of the Queen. They held that the application for quashing the indictment must be refused. Mr. Baron Pollock and Mr. Justice Hawkins concurred.

The jury was then sworn, and Mr. Avory formally opened the pleadings, alleging that the defendants, in the months of November and December, 1895, were unlawfully engaged in the preparation of a military expedition to proceed against the dominions of a friendly State—to wit, the South African Republic; in assisting and fitting out the expedition, and also that they were unlawfully employed in various capacities in the expedition. To these charges they had pleaded "Not Guilty."

Sir Richard Webster then proceeded to open the case on behalf of the Crown. He said that it would be necessary to explain the relations of Her Majesty's Government to the South African Republic. These relations were controlled by conventions and treaties, the bearing of which was familiar, and was, no doubt, known to the defendants. The territory known as the Transvaal, or South African Republic, had, after certain chequered incidents in its history, been annexed to Her Majesty's dominions, and by the Convention of April 5th, 1881, Her Majesty's Commissioners, acting on behalf of Her Majesty, undertook to guarantee complete self-government to the Transvaal, subject to the suzerainty of the Queen, and subject to certain other conditions into which he need not go. The important point the jury had to remember was, that from July, 1881, the South African Republic was to have complete self-government, and that was guaranteed on behalf of the Queen. On October 29th, 1889, a company was incorporated—the British South Africa Company—to which a charter was granted by the Queen.

The defendants were all gentlemen of high position in connection with the Chartered Company or the Bechuanaland Border Police, and must have known, and certainly did know, of the relations between Her Majesty's Government and the South African Republic. Coming to his narrative as to what occurred in November and December, 1895, Sir R. Webster proceeded to describe the "raid," from the

THE LATE MR. B. I. BARNATO,
SENIOR MEMBER OF THE LEGISLATIVE ASSEMBLY FOR KIMBERLEY.

departure of the two columns from Mafeking and Pitsani to the defeat at Krugersdorp. A man observed the party cross the border, and on informing Major White that he should report what was going on, met with the retort, "You can do what you like. The wires are cut." And their Lordships would see that the wires were cut subsequent to the closing of the telegraph office on that (Sunday) morning, December 29th, and undoubtedly they were cut by direction of those concerned in this expedition. Counsel argued that beyond question the expedition was deliberately planned in secrecy with the intention of proceeding from Mafeking for the purpose of conducting military operations against the Transvaal Republic. He next brought forward certain facts and documents to show that Mafeking and Pitsani were within British dominions. No one could over-estimate the enormous responsibility which rested on the law officers in this case, but by the weight of evidence which he should submit to the Court he should ask their Lordships to say that an unlawful expedition had been fitted out to make war on a friendly State in the manner he had just indicated.

After the witnesses had given evidence the Lord Chief Justice commenced his summing-up.

In reviewing the evidence of the Transvaalers his Lordship said:—

"The men, subjects of the Transvaal, who gave evidence before you, gave their evidence without any kind of restraint, without any animus, and in a perfectly straightforward manner."

Referring to the letter of invitation said to have been addressed to Dr. Jameson, he said:—

"This letter speaks of no oppression contrary to the law; it spoke of no injustice in not carrying out the law. A large number of Uitlanders had not got the franchise, had not got a fair share in the making of the laws of the country of their adoption, and which their number, their wealth, and their property interest entitled them to; but the letter pointed to no emergency, pointed to no threat of massacre, still less of a threat of attack upon the women and children. Assuming the letter set forth real grievances, ought it to have been addressed to the heads of a trading company? Her Majesty had her representatives in the Transvaal. An appeal to the latter would have been intelligible, but not one to Dr. Jameson."

Dealing with Dr. Jameson's protest that they were only attempting to obtain ordinary political rights for the people of Johannesburg, he asked with much emotion, and his voice tremulous with feeling—

"What had Dr. Jameson to do with political rights, or with the settlers on the Rand?"

In concluding his summing-up, Lord Russell said it was obvious that Dr. Jameson and the others were misinformed as to the attitude and temper of the people of Johannesburg. He expected at least two thousand armed men to assist him.

His Lordship next reviewed the documents and telegrams presented in the case, and closed by putting four questions before the jury:—

Firstly, were the defendants engaged in the preparation of a military expedition against a friendly State?

Secondly, did all the defendants assist in the preparation of the expedition, and did they aid and abet in its furtherance?

Thirdly, were the defendants, or any of them, employed in any capacity in the expedition?

Fourthly, with regard to Pitsani, did the Queen exercise dominion in that district in which it was situated?

The jury retired to consider their verdict.

On their return, after seventy minutes absence, the foreman said the jury found all the questions against the defendants.

The Lord Chief Justice then directed the jury to return a verdict of guilty on all the counts.

The foreman explained that the jury desired to add a rider to their verdict, having reference to the provocation given by the alarmist statements issued from Johannesburg.

Sir Edward Clarke rose, but the Lord Chief Justice refused to allow him to interpose between himself and the jury.

The foreman said, although the jury had answered the

[*To face page* 246.

CARTRIDGES, VULTURES FEATHERS, SPENT BULLET, RAMROD,
AND NECKTIE FROM DOORNKOP.

(*From a photograph by C. H. B. Lovegrove.*)

questions in the affirmative, they could not agree as to a verdict of guilty or not guilty.

The Lord Chief Justice said they had already given a verdict of guilty.

Sir Edward Clarke, after making a motion to stay judgment, permitted judgment to be given without protest.

The Lord Chief Justice then pronounced the sentence of the Court as follows:—

Dr. Jameson to fifteen months' imprisonment; Colonel Sir John Willoughby to ten months'; Major White to seven months'; Colonel Grey, Major Coventry, and Colonel White to five months' each—all without hard labour.

On the conclusion of the trial Dr. Jameson and his fellow-prisoners took leave of their friends in the ante-room of the Court.

The arrangements for their removal were not completed till 8 o'clock. When these were at length finished, the prisoners and their escort tried to leave quietly by a side exit, but an enormous crowd quickly gathered. The prisoners were received with wild cheering, hats and handkerchiefs were waved, and many shook Dr. Jameson by the hand.

Mr. Hawksley, Solicitor of the Chartered Company, Dr. Harris, and Lord Annaly accompanied Dr. Jameson in the cab to Holloway Prison.

Dr. Jameson remarked to a friend after judgment had been pronounced: "Well, it might have been worse."

While in Holloway Prison all the prisoners were treated as first-class misdemeanants; but they were afterwards transferred to Wormwood Scrubbs and treated as ordinary prisoners.

Major Coventry was placed in the infirmary, owing to ill-health.

All felt their position most keenly. They were shaved, according to the regulations, and put in prison garb.

Lord Loch interviewed Dr. Jameson in gaol on the 30th July.

The next day, acting on the advice of the Home Secretary, the Queen decided to extend her clemency to Dr. Jameson and his fellow-prisoners, and grant them the treatment of first-class misdemeanants.

They accordingly returned to Holloway the same day.

So finishes the great drama of the Uitlander movement of 1896. The result, so far, has been to strengthen the Government of the South African Republic, not only pecuniarily, but also in power and prestige; and the President, by his crowning act of mercy, has earned the sobriquet of Mr. Barnato, who described him as "the Grand Old Man of the South African Republic."

THE BLACK LIST OF 1896, AS AFFECTING SOUTH AFRICA.

1. The Johannesburg Crisis (the Jameson Raid).

2. The Fatal Railway Disaster at Glencoe Junction (forty killed).

3. The Dynamite Disaster at Fordsburg (some hundreds killed).

4. The Matabele Outbreak (hundreds of Europeans massacred by Natives).

5. The Rinderpest (thousands of cattle have died and are dying).

6. The *Drummond Castle* wrecked (250 drowned).

7. Locust Plague.

8. Drought.

Whatever may be in store in the future, I trust that the prayers offered in all the churches and places of worship, throughout the Transvaal, on the Day of Humiliation (June 7th, 1896), may be heard, and that the Divine vengeance may be stayed.

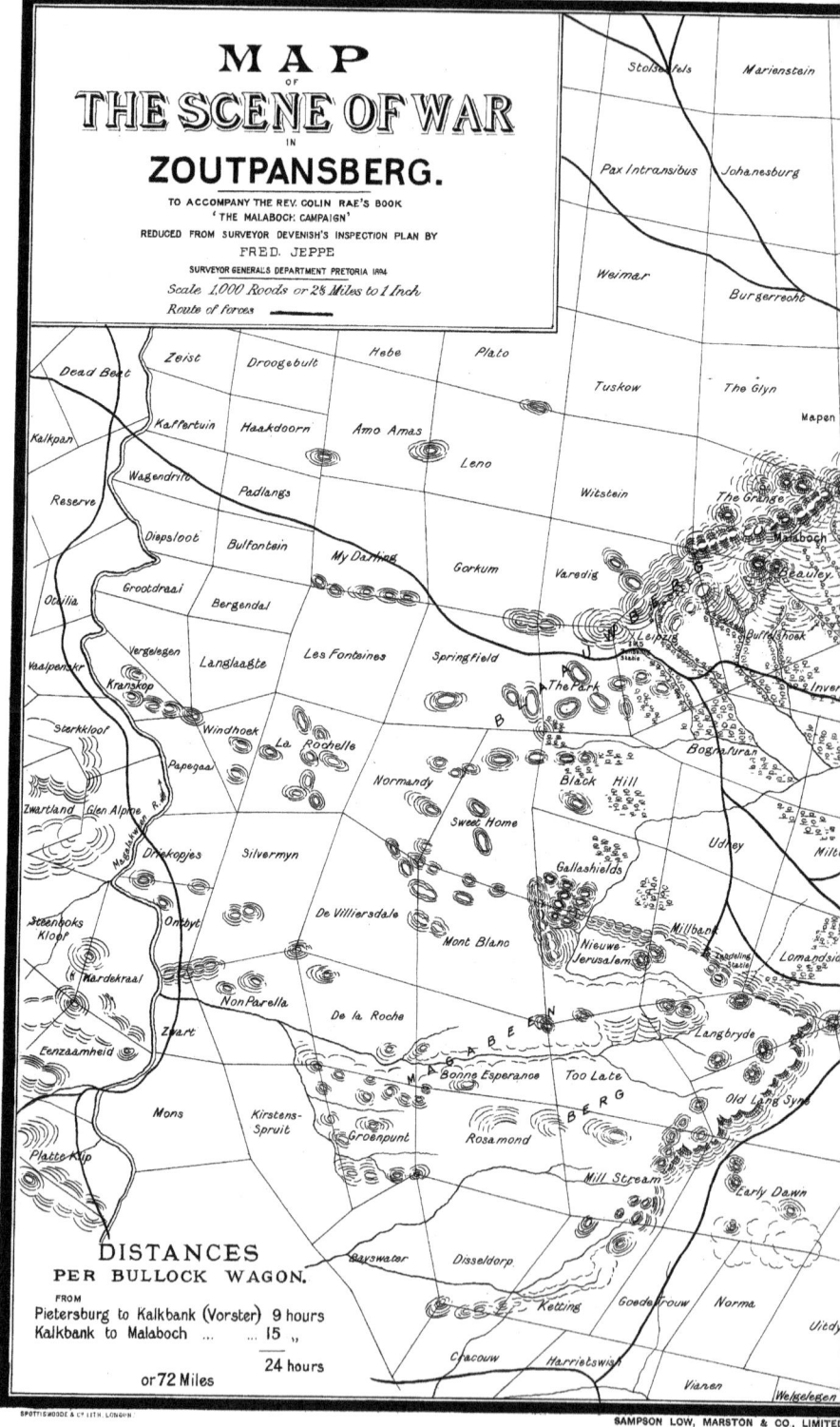

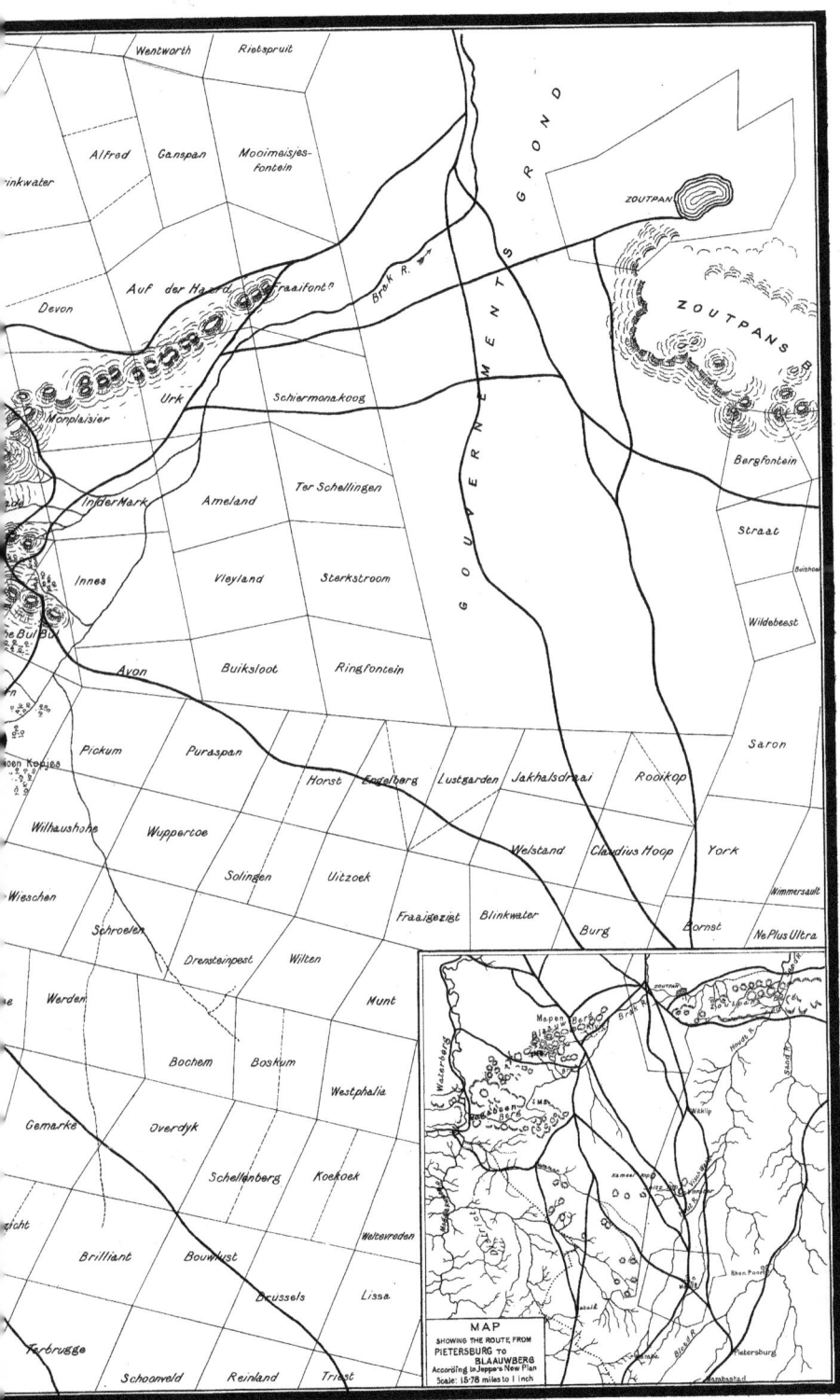

www.ingramcontent.com/pod-product-compliance
Lightning Source LLC
Chambersburg PA
CBHW051035160426
43193CB00010B/945